teach® yourself

flash mx 2004

mac bride

teach yourself

flash mx 2004

mac bride

for over 60 years, more than 40 million people have learnt over 750 subjects the **teach yourself** way, with impressive results.

be where you want to be with **teach yourself**

For UK order enquiries: please contact Bookpoint Ltd, 130 Milton Park, Abingdon, Oxon OX14 4SB. Telephone: +44 (0)1235 827720. Fax: +44 (0)1235 400454. Lines are open 09.00–18.00, Monday to Saturday, with a 24-hour message answering service. Details about our titles and how to order are available at www.teachyourself.co.uk.

For USA order enquiries: please contact McGraw-Hill Customer Services, PO Box 545, Blacklick, OH 43004-0545, USA. Telephone: 1-800-722-4726. Fax: 1-614-755-5645.

For Canada order enquiries: please contact McGraw-Hill Ryerson Ltd, 300 Water St, Whitby, Ontario L1N 9B6, Canada. Telephone: 905 430 5000. Fax: 905 430 5020.

Long renowned as the authoritative source for self-guided learning – with more than 40 million copies sold worldwide – the **teach yourself** series includes over 300 titles in the fields of languages, crafts, hobbies, business, computing and education.

British Library Cataloguing in Publication Data: a catalogue record for this title is available from The British Library.

Library of Congress Catalog Card Number: on file.

First published in UK 2005 by Hodder Education, 338 Euston Road, London, NW1 3BH.

First published in US 2005 by Contemporary Books, a Division of the McGraw-Hill Companies, 1 Prudential Plaza, 130 East Randolph Street, Chicago, IL 60601 USA.

The **teach yourself** name is a registered trademark of Hodder Headline.

Typeset by MacDesign, Southampton

Printed in Great Britain for Hodder Education, a division of Hodder Headline, 338 Euston Road, London NW1 3BH, by Cox & Wyman Ltd, Reading, Berkshire.

Hodder Headline's policy is to use papers that are natural, renewable and recyclable products and made from wood grown in sustainable forests. The logging and manufacturing processes are expected to conform to the environmental regulations of the country of origin.

Impression number   10 9 8 7 6 5 4 3 2 1

Year   2009 2008 2007 2006 2005

v

contents

preface

Flash MX 2004 is the latest version of the world's leading web page animation software – though in this version it will do far more than just animate text and images on a web page. You can use this Flash to produce interactive online forms, front-ends to databases, tests and other educational software, and presentations, amongst other things. And the resulting movies can be run not only in standard web browsers but also in pocket PCs, and a wide range of mobile devices.

This book concentrates on the core of Flash – its animation facilities. It aims to provide clear and simple coverage of the concepts and techniques involved in drawing and animating text and images. ActionScript, Flash's programming language is introduced, but in outline only. It is a large and complex system and needs a whole book to itself to be treated properly!

No special knowledge or skills are needed to start learning Flash. I'm assuming that you have a basic familiarity with computers – you can find your way round menus and dialog boxes, control a mouse and install software from a CD. If you can write HTML code, you will find that useful when you are finishing off your web pages, and if you have any experience of programming, that will help when you start work with ActionScript.

What you really need to produce good Flash movies is time, energy, enthusiasm and ideas. Working with Flash is hugely enjoyable and can be challenging, which is part of the enjoyment. Have fun!

Mac Bride
Southampton, 2005

01

animation in a Flash

In this chapter you will learn:

- about the Flash environment
- how to manage the panels
- about the startup options
- how to make a simple movie
- how to set preferences
- about the Help system

1.1 Flash MX

Flash MX 2004 is the latest version of the world's leading web animation system. It can be used to produce an almost infinite variety of active and interactive graphic, text, sound and video experiences, ranging from simple moving logos through menus, demos and quizzes to complex, fast-moving games. It has sophisticated 'tweening' techniques that can create the images between given start and end points, so that you can move or resize an image smoothly, or even change one shape into an other. At the time of writing, an estimated 1 million developers, designers and web professionals use this or earlier versions of Flash, and over 95% of all web browsers can view Flash movies.

The concepts behind Flash, its tools and its techniques are all straightforward – even if some are not immediately obvious – and can be mastered quickly. It only takes a few hours to grasp enough of the basics to produce an animated display – though rather more hours of practice to really get to know your way around the system. The time-consuming part of Flash development, as with any creative work, is thinking up the ideas and designs, and producing the images that are to be animated. If you are coming to Flash from an art or graphics background, you will have a head start in this respect.

To make your movies interactive, rather than merely active, you need to learn a new and different set of skills and concepts. ActionScript is a programming language, similar to JavaScript. At the simplest, you can attach a single instruction to a button or other object, perhaps to start a new movie within the movie, to connect to an Internet address or to calculate a result. At the other end of the scale, you can use ActionScript to write games, simulations and demonstrations.

1.2 The Flash environment

The Flash environment has several major components and a lot of minor ones, some of which need to be visible all the time, while others can be opened and closed when needed. In fact, there are so many components that visibility can be a problem. Run Flash now, identify the components and learn how to manage your screen display so that you can see what you are doing and can reach the tools you need.

The application window and movie windows

As with many Windows applications, you can have any number of files open at the same time in Flash. Each movie runs in its own window, and you can manage these and move between them exactly as you can with multiple documents in Word.

At the top of the application window is the usual menu bar. The Main toolbar, with buttons for the common commands, is turned off by default, but can be turned on from the **Window** menu.

Timeline

Movie window

Toolbox   Stage   Work area   Color mixer

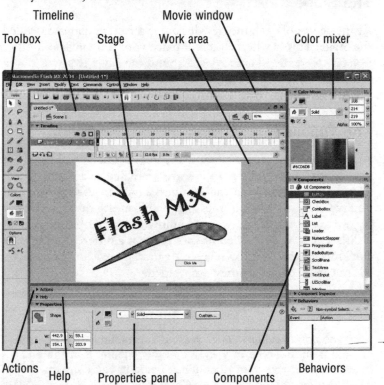

Actions Help   Properties panel   Components   Behaviors

The Flash window normally fills the whole screen – and it needs to as there are a lot of elements. The default layout includes panels that you will probably not need at first. A panel can be expanded or shrunk back to its title bar by clicking on the name or the arrow beside it.

The Toolbox

This is usually on the lefthand side of the application window, and contains the drawing tools. When a tool is selected, if it has options, these are shown at the bottom of the toolbox. When you have finished the drawing stage of your project and are working on the timing of the animation, or are writing Action-Script, the toolbox can be closed to free up its space.

To show or hide the Toolbox:

• Open the **Window** menu and click **Tools**.

The Stage

At the centre of each movie window is a rectangular area called the Stage. This is where you will place your drawings and other objects to create your movies. Around the stage is a work area which you can use for temporary storage while you are developing your movies.

The Timeline

At the top of the movie window is the Timeline, which is where you control how your graphics are animated over time. There are two aspects to this: the numbers relate to the frames, and you typically run at 12 frames a second; beneath the frame counter are the *layers*. If you want to animate several objects, each in a different way, at a different speed and at a different time, then each must be set in its own layer. At first, there is only one layer. More can be added as they are needed.

Getting Flash

If you don't yet have Flash, you can download it on a 30-day trial from its home at www.macromedia.com. If at the end of the trial, you want to continue using it, you can activate the software by paying the $420 (£240) price.

If you are a teacher or student in a school or college, you qualify for an educational discount and can buy single copies at around £80 or get a site licence at a much reduced rate.

The panels

Most of the options, for formatting text and lines, setting colours and fine-tuning the layout and other aspects of the design, are managed through panels. Panels are also used to hold the tools for developing interactive programs. Initially, seven panels are open, arranged on the right and at the bottom of the screen.

Panels can be opened and closed as they are needed, and floated to anywhere on screen. Some can be docked, others are always floaters (and those which can be docked, don't always go where they are told). It's a tricky business finding the optimum balance of convenience and visibility. The default layout leaves a fairly small area of screen for the stage, and includes elements that you don't normally need until later stages of movie development. As a general rule, close any that aren't in use – they are simple enough to re-open when you need them.

While you are designing and animating your movie, the most important panels are Properties, which show the options and settings for the currently selected object or tool, and Color Mixer. It's also useful to have Help at hand – but floating, and enlarged, not docked at the bottom of the screen.

The Actions and Behavior panels will be needed when you start to add interactivity to your movie; the Components and Component Inspector panels are used when creating forms. All of these could be closed at this point.

To shrink or expand a panel:

◆ Click on the name or the arrow to its left.

To close a panel:

◆ Right-click on the panel's title bar and select **Close Panel**.

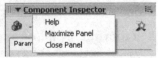

Windows PCs and Macs

To save space, I have only given instructions in Windows format. They are exactly the same on Macintoshes except: for Right-click use Control-click, instead of [Ctrl] + [key] use [Command] + [key], and for [Enter] use [Return].

To display a panel:

1 Open the **Window** menu.

2 To open the **Properties** or **Library** panels, click on their names.

3 To open other panels, point to **Design, Development** or **Other Panels** and select from the set that appears.

Window	Help	
New Window	Ctrl+Alt+K	
Toolbars	▶	
✓ Properties	Ctrl+F3	
✓ Timeline	Ctrl+Alt+T	
✓ Tools	Ctrl+F2	
Library	Ctrl+L	
Design Panels	▶	Align Ctrl+K
Development Panels	▶	✓ Color Mixer Shift+F9
Other Panels	▶	Color Swatches Ctrl+F9
		Info Ctrl+I
Hide Panels	F4	Scene Shift+F2
Panel Sets	▶	Transform Ctrl+T
Save Panel Layout...		
Cascade		
Tile		
✓ 1 Untitled-1*		

You may find that there are certain layouts which you use regularly for different types of work. Rather than fiddling around setting up the layout each time, you can save it, then apply the layout whenever you need it.

To save a layout:

1 Open the panels as required.

2 Drag the panels into the most convenient places.

3 From the **Window** menu select **Save Panel Layout...**

Save Panel Layout		
Name:	design layout	OK
		Cancel

4 Type in a meaningful name.

To reapply a layout:

1 Open the **Window** menu, point to **Panel Sets** and select the layout.

Training Layout

The Panel Sets includes a layout specially designed for new users. This has only the Properties at the bottom of the screen, and the Help panel open, but moved to the right. An alternative is to float the Help panel out of its dock, expand it to a workable size and drag it to a convenient area of the screen. It doesn't matter if it partly obscures other things, as it can be shrunk out of the way when not needed.

1.3 Startup options

When you start Flash, and when you have closed down all open documents, you will be presented with this display, from where you can open a document or start a new one.

- **Open a Recent Item** lists the last ten files that you have been working on.

- **Create New** Flash Document lets you start from scratch. This is the option we will be using.

• **Create from Template** can be a quick way to start a document. Some of the templates simply set an appropriate page size; others have a lot of the style and structure in place, and need mainly content from you. When you select one of the folders at the start-up display, the **New from Template** dialog box opens, and this is where you select a template.

A template can get a new document off to a flying start, but these are not an alternative to learning Flash! You need a good grasp of Flash to be able to make full use fo them.

1.4 Your first movie

Just to show how easy it can be, we're going to make a movie. It won't be a great one, but it will demonstrate a few key concepts and techniques of Flash movie-making. There are four stages:

• Plan and design the movie

• Create the images and other content

• Animate the images

• Test and publish the movie.

Plan and design the movie

In this case, this stage will be very quick and easy, but in a proper movie, it can be one of the most time-consuming parts of the process. You need to think through *exactly* what you want it to do and how it will look. What our movie will do is make a ball bounce. The ball will be round, smallish and whatever colour happens to be selected by default.

Create the images

1 If you have a blank stage in front of you, move to step 2, otherwise open the **File** menu and select **New**.

2 At the **New Document** dialog box, select **Flash Document** on the **General** tab.

3 Notice the document properties. The default movie will run in a 550 × 400 window, on a white background at 12 frames per second. You can change any of these. Click the **Size** button and make the window 400 × 300 pixels.

```
Document Properties

    Dimensions:  [ 400 px ]  (width)   x   [ 300 px ]  (height)
         Match:  [ Printer ]  [ Contents ]  [ Default ]
Background color:  [ _ ]
    Frame rate:  [ 12 ]  fps
   Ruler units:  [ Pixels ▼ ]

          [ Make Default ]        [ OK ]   [ Cancel ]
```

4 Click on the **Oval** tool in the Toolbox.

5 Point to somewhere near the bottom of the stage. The cursor will now be a cross-hair icon.

6 Click to the top left of where you want the circle to start. Hold down [Shift] (this makes it draw a circle rather than oval) and drag down and to the right.

7 An outline of the circle will appear and change as you drag. Release the mouse button when the circle is the right size – about as big as your thumbnail.

Save it!

Before you go any further, save your work. I know that it's only taken you two minutes to get this far, but it's good to get into the habit of saving early and saving often. You'll thank me for this one day, when the PC crashes on you, or you delete a chunk of a movie and can't undo the deletion!

Open the File menu, select Save As, and save the file with a suitable name in an appropriate folder. Notice that the file has the extension '.fla'.

Animate the images

The ball that you have just drawn is on frame 1 of the movie. We now need to create more frames showing the same ball, but in different positions, to give the illusion of movement. There are two ways to do this:

• The hard way – create each frame separately. You have to do this where the movements are irregular or the image changes in an irregular fashion.

• The easy way – create another frame further along the Timeline when the image reaches its end point (or its new shape), and get Flash to create the frames in between.

We'll use the easy way. First we need to adjust the drawing. At the moment, it has two components – and outline and a fill. If we turn these into a single object, it will be easier to animate.

1 Click 🖘 the Selection tool.

2 Drag a rectangle to enclose the circle and select it – it will take on a fine dot pattern to show that it is selected.

3 Open the **Modify** menu and select **Group**. A thin blue square will appear around it. This is how Flash indicates that a grouped image is selected.

Now to animate it.

1 In the Timeline, click on layer 1 at frame 10.

2 Press [F6]. You have made this into a *keyframe*.

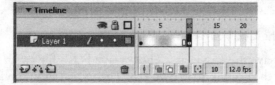

3 The ball should be visible, at the bottom of the stage, and it should still be selected – if not, click on it now.

4 Drag the ball straight up towards the top of the stage.

5 Right-click on layer 1 anywhere between frames 1 and 10.

6 Select **Create Motion Tween** from the pop-up menu. Flash will change the position of the ball on the intervening frames, moving it steadily up.

7 Open the **Control** menu and select **Rewind**. Frame 1 will be selected in the Timeline.

8 Open the **Control** menu and select **Play**.

That's got the ball up in the air. Let's get it down again. Repeat the last set of steps with these two changes:

• Create the new keyframe at Frame 20.

• And move the ball down to the bottom again in that frame.

When you play the revised movie, the ball should go up and down once.

Test the movie

Playing a movie inside the Flash environment is good for testing that the animation works, but you need to get off the stage and away from the clutter of the development environment to really see your movie. The Test Movie routine will do that for you.

* Open the **Control** menu and select **Test Movie**.

Flash will save the movie as a Shockwave Flash file (with a .swf extension) then run it in its own tab. The movie should play in a loop – this is the default setting. When you get tired of watching the ball bounce up and down, close the tab or switch back to the design tab.

Switch to Design tab   Close the tab

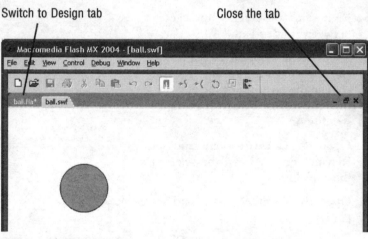

When you play the movie, the new .swf tab fills the Flash window and you can't do much except watch it, as long as it is there!

1.5 Preferences

The preferences allow you to fine-tune the Flash environment to suit your way of working. At first, few of these will make much sense, and all should be left at their default settings until you understand what difference they make. However, you will soon start to see what they are about and you should know about the preferences so that you can adjust them when you are ready.

Preferences

General | Editing | Clipboard | Warnings | ActionScript

General

Undo levels: 100 — If you are short of memory, reduce the number of **Undo** levels

Printing options: ☐ Disable PostScript

Selection options: ☑ Shift select — Leave this on – you'll see why in Chapter 2

☑ Show tooltips — Also best left on for the time being

Panel options: ☐ Disable panel docking

Timeline options: ☐ Disable timeline docking
☐ Span based selection
☐ Named anchor on Scene

Highlight color: ◉ Use this color
○ Use layer color

Font mapping default: _sans

On launch: ○ Show Start Page
○ New document
◉ Last documents open — What do you want to see when you start Flash?
○ No document

OK | Cancel

To change the preferences:

1 Open the **Edit** menu and select **Preferences…**

2 Click the required tab to bring it to the top. There are five:

General – these options configure aspects of the Flash environment.

Editing – these control how Flash displays and interprets your freehand drawing. We'll look at these in Chapter 2.

Clipboard – these relate to graphics being copied into and out of Flash.

Warnings – these will alert you to possible conflicts. They are all on by default – and are probably best left on.

ActionScript – these are mainly for formatting the code.

1.6 Help

Flash MX offers you lots of Help – the problem is finding the bit you need. There are two parts to the system:

• The main set of Help pages, which are split into several books including Getting Started, Using Flash, Using ActionScript, AcriptScript Language Reference and Using Components.

• The How Do I... pages that give detailed practical advice on a selection of specific jobs in Flash and ActionScript.

Both sets of pages are managed through the same window and are accessed in the same way.

The Help contents

1 First, start the Help system. Open the Help menu and select Help or How Do I...

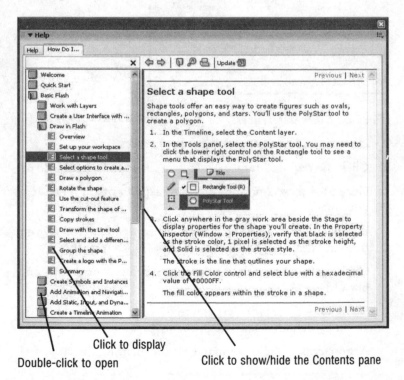

Double-click to open   Click to display

Click to show/hide the Contents pane

2 If the Contents pane is not visible, click on the handle on the divider bar.

3 Double-click on a 'book' to open it up.

4 Click on a topic to display it in the main frame.

5 Text in blue carries a link to a related topic – click on it if you want to read it.

6 Use the ⇦ ⇨ arrows to go backwards and forwards through pages that you have already visited.

7 Use the **Previous** and **Next** links to open the adjacent pages in the Contents list.

Help Search

1 Start the Help system, if necessary.

2 Click on the 🔍 icon in the navigation bar.

Keep keywords simple   Contents   Search

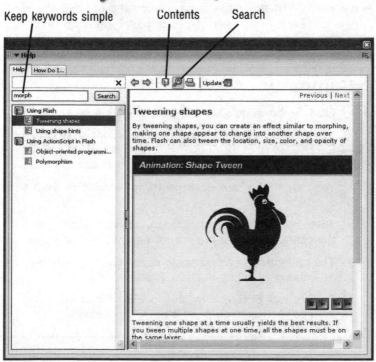

3 Type one or more words to describe what you are looking for.

4 Click **Search**.

♦ Searching in **How Do I...** generally produces very few results – only the basics are covered here. A search in the main pages can produce too many possible topics.

♦ If you do not find what you need, go back to step 3 and try different keywords.

5 Select a topic and click **Display**. The Help page will appear in the main frame of the browser.

Help where you can see it

The default position for the Help panel produces a shallow display, with only two or three lines visible at a time. This is useless for most purposes. The Training Layout is better, but the panel is too narrow to show the contents/search pane and the Help page at the same time. Float the Help panel out of its dock and make the window a decent size.

Summary

♦ Flash is the world's leading web animation system.

♦ The Flash window has many elements, not all of which are needed all of the time. Panels can be resized, moved or closed if not needed to free up screen space.

♦ You can start a new document from scratch or from a template.

♦ There are four stages in making a movie: design, create the content, animate the images and publish the movie.

♦ The preferences can be set to adjust Flash to your way of working.

♦ There's lots of Help available in Flash, though finding the specific Help you need is not always easy.

drawing basics

In this chapter you will learn:

- about raster and vector graphics
- how to draw a line
- about the ruler, guides and grid
- about the tools that can be used for selection
- how to transform drawings
- how to set colours
- about groups

2.1 Vector and raster graphics

There are essentially two ways of defining images on a computer system: raster graphics and vector graphics.

* In raster graphics, an image is defined by storing the colour and intensity of each individual pixel. Producing a picture with raster graphics software, such as Windows Paint (a very aptly-named program) is like putting paint on a canvas. Once you have drawn a line or shape, you can paint over it or erase it, but you cannot edit it. Each new line becomes an integral part of the whole image.

* In vector graphics, an image is the sum of its component lines and shapes, each of which is defined mathematically, in terms of position, size, angle, curves, colour, fill pattern, etc. With a picture produced by a vector graphics system, such as the drawing tools in Word, you can, at any point, pick up a component and change its size, angle or whatever. However much you distort or enlarge a shape, it retains the same sharp edges and smooth curves. In contrast, if you enlarge a raster image, it gets jagged and blocky.

Flash is a vector-based system, like Word's drawing tools, but far more sophisticated and giving you far more control over the final appearance of any line or shape.

The first thing you need to realise is that there is more to a shape than meets the eye. You can see this most clearly if you look carefully at a rectangle with rounded corners – and we'll draw one in the next chapter, after we've covered the basic concepts and techniques. The rectangle appears to be a solid unit:

But in fact, it is a composite of four sides, four curves and a fill – which is a solid unit.

Each of these components can be selected and edited separately. And in fact, the readiness with which shapes separate into lines and fills, and lines separate into sections, can be irritating at times. We'll get back to this shortly when we look at selecting.

The second thing to note is that you can look at and edit the vectors that define the lines. A straight line is defined by an anchor point at each end, and these can be dragged to change the length or angle of the line. A curve is defined by anchor points at each end and a third in between. By moving the points and by changing the direction of the tangent (the line that runs through each point), you can change the nature of the curve.

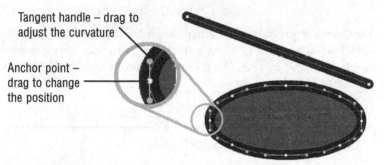

Tangent handle – drag to
adjust the curvature

Anchor point –
drag to change
the position

A line has only two points; an oval is treated as a series of curves.

The best way to get to grips with drawing in Flash, is do it, so let's get started. First, we'll create some basic lines and shapes – sticking to the simplest drawing tools – then we'll explore the selecting and editing techniques.

2.2 Drawing the line

The **Line** tool is one of the simplest to use and produces the simplest object.

1 Click ✏ the **Line** tool in the Toolbox. The cursor will change to the crosshair icon.

2 Click where you want the line to start.

3 Drag to draw the line. A thin guide line will show you where the line will apppear when you release the mouse button. Notice the circle at the end of the line (beneath the crosshairs).

Large circle when the line
is horizontal or vertical...

Normal tiny
circle at end

... or touching a line

When the line is exactly horizontal or vertical, or when the end is over an existing line, the circle becomes larger. This can be a useful way of telling when you are in the right place.

4   Release the mouse button when the line is in the right place.

The line will probably be rather thin – the default thickness is only 1 point – which gives us a small target for our experiments in selecting and editing. We'll erase the line, increase the thickness setting and start again.

5   Open the **Edit** menu and select **Undo**.

Undo/Redo

Edit > Undo (or 🔄 or the [Ctrl] + [Z] keystroke) undoes the effect of the last action, and you can keep on undoing to roll back a whole series of actions. This is mainly there so that you can correct any mistakes – removing unwanted objects or restoring those deleted in error – but it also gives you freedom to experiment. If something doesn't work, you can always go back to where you were.

If you get carried away, and undo too many moves, Edit > Redo (🔄 or [Ctrl] + [Y]) will undo the undoing.

Stroke settings

The stroke – the appearance of the line – has three settings: style, thickness and colour. These are all controlled on the **Properties** panel when the Line tool is active, or a line has been selected.

1   If you cannot see the **Properties** panel, open the **Window** menu and select **Properties**.

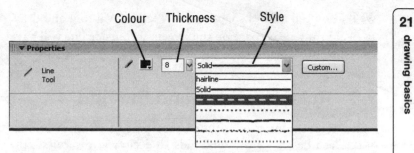

Colour   Thickness   Style

2 *To change the style*, drop down the list at the top of the tab and click on a sample line. A solid line would probably be best for the experiments in this chapter, but please yourself.

3 *To change the thickness*, type in a new number or click the arrow to the right of the field. A slider will appear, push this up or down to set the thickness – 4 or 5 points would be a good thickness for our purposes.

4 *To change the colour*, click the down arrow to the right of the colour swatch and select from the palette that appears. Any colour will do just now, as long as there is a good contrast with the background.

Draw three or four lines with your new, more visible, settings. Make sure that one line crosses another – it will demonstrate an important lesson.

Custom lines

The Custom button leads to the Stroke Style dialog box where you can customise your line in an infinite variety of ways. Every style has its own set of options. Explore them.

Stroke Style				☒
	Type:	Stipple ▾		OK
	Dot size:	Medium ▾		Cancel
	Dot variation:	Random Sizes ▾		
☐ Zoom 4x	Density:	Dense ▾		
Thickness: 4 ▾ pts				
☑ Sharp corners				

We'll also need a solid shape. Click ◯ the **Oval** tool and draw an oval in any clear space on the screen. Its outside line will have the same Stroke settings as the straight lines.

2.3 Rulers, guides and the grid

Accurate positioning is an important part of effective animation. Flash has three optional aids to accuracy: the rulers, the guides and the grid.

The rulers

These mark off the co-ordinates (in pixels), from the top left of the stage. When you are drawing an object, the position of the crosshairs cursor is shown on the rulers, allowing you to set the position and size accurately.

View Insert Modify Text Commands

Go to	▶
Zoom In	Ctrl+=
Zoom Out	Ctrl+-
Magnification	▶
Preview Mode	▶
✓ Work Area	Ctrl+Shift+W
✓ Rulers	Ctrl+Alt+Shift+R
Grid	▶
Guides	▶
Snapping	▶
Hide Edges	Ctrl+H
Show Shape Hints	Ctrl+Alt+H

♦ The rulers can be turned on or off by opening the **View** menu and clicking **Rulers**.

The guides

The guides are faint lines which can be pulled out from the rulers and placed on the stage, so that objects can be aligned with them.

To use the guides:

1 Turn on the rulers.

2 Point to the side or top ruler, then drag onto the stage. A line will appear. Release the mouse button when it is in place. If you need to move a guide later, drag it.

♦ *To hide (or show) the guides,* open the **View** menu, point to **Guides** and toggle **Show guides** on or off.

♦ *To lock the guides,* so that they cannot be moved accidentally, open the **View** menu, point to **Guides** and tick **Lock guides**. Clear the tick to unlock them.

Start of current drawing   Current cursor position

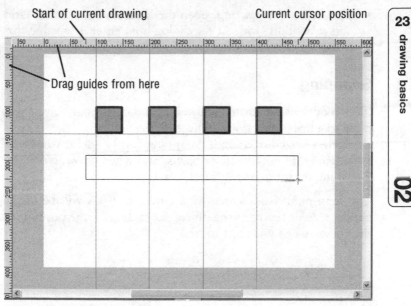

Using guides to align objects

- *To change the colour of the guides*, open the **View** menu, point to **Guides** and click **Edit guides**. Select a new colour at the dialog box.

The grid

The grid is a set of regularly-spaced vertical and horizontal lines that can be used instead of, or as well as, the guides.

- *To turn the grid on or off*, open the **View** menu, point to **Grid** and toggle **Show grid** on or off.

- *To edit the grid spacing*, open the **View** menu, point to **Grid** and select **Edit Grid**. At the dialog box, enter new values for the spaces between the vertical and/or horizontal lines.

Snapping

If **Snap** options are turned on, points and corners of objects will jump to a line or junction on the grid, the guides or other objects when they are close enough. Snapping can be useful when you are aligning new or existing objects, and when drawing objects, if it is important that they meet exactly.

The snap point is indicated by a circle, and this will be at the corner, side or centre of the object depending on the position of the cursor when you start to drag.

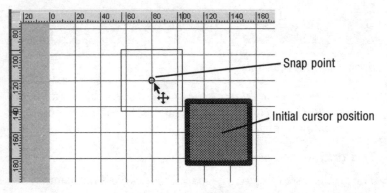

Snap point

Initial cursor position

- *Turn snap on or off* from the **View > Snapping** submenu.

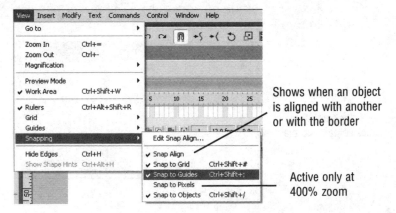

Shows when an object is aligned with another or with the border

Active only at 400% zoom

2.4 The Selection tool

There are three selecting tools in Flash. First, the Selection tool.

1 Click on ▶ the **Selection** tool. The cursor will change to a black arrow with a small box beside it.

2 *To select a single object*, click on it.

Clicking here selects the top part of the line

If you click on a line which crosses another, it will be selected up to the crossing point.

If you click on the oval, you will select either the fill or the line, depending upon exactly where you clicked.

3 *To select multiple objects*, hold down [**Shift**] while you click on them.

Shift Select

There is a Shift Select option on the General tab of the Preferences dialog box. If this is on, you must hold down [Shift] to select multiple objects. If it is off, you can select multiple objects by simply clicking on them – but you cannot deselect an unwanted one without deselecting them all.

---

4 *To select all the objects – or parts of objects – in an area*, imagine a rectangle that would enclose them all, then click at one of its corners and drag across to the opposite one.

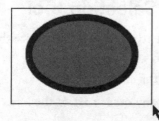

Use the rectangle approach to select a filled shape or a group of objects.

When (part of) an object is selected, it is shown with a faint crosshatch

If the rectangle cuts across an object, only those parts inside the rectangle are selected

Working with selected objects

Once an object has been selected, you can move it, delete it or change its settings.

To move an object:

1 Select the object(s) – or the part(s) that you want.

2 Click anywhere on the selected object and drag into place.

3 Click on the background of the stage to deselect the objects.

   You must select an object before you try to move it. If you just try to click and drag a line, you will bend it – see below.

Snap to it

The Selection tool has an important option. When the Snap to Objects modifier is on, a little circle will appear at the corner or centre of the selected object when it is in position to connect exactly with another object.

2.5 Editing with the Selection tool

If you move the arrow cursor close to a line you will notice that it changes.

♦ It looks like ↳ when it is near the end of a line

♦ and like this ↳ when it is near any other part of the line.

The icons are there to remind you of what will happen if you click and drag on the line at that point.

Drag on the line

If you drag on the main part of a line, it will bend. No matter where on the line you start to drag, the whole line will be curved.

> Remember **Undo** – curves are notoriously difficult to get right first time

Drag on the end

If you click on the end of a line, you can drag it to a new place. Straight lines will stay straight, so only their length or angle can be changed. Curved lines will be recurved, and as before, the whole line will be affected.

[Ctrl] – drag

If you hold down [Ctrl] while you drag, it changes the effect.

[Ctrl] – drag on a straight line will create a new corner at that point, with straight lines back to the original ends.

[Ctrl] – drag on a curved line will create a new point, with new curves on either side.

Smooth and Straighten

The Selection tool has two more options. These are only active when a line is selected:

⤴ **Smooth** will turn a rough line into a smooth curve

⤵ **Straighten** will turn a curve into a straight line.

Click the buttons to adjust the selected line.

Practise!

Start with an oval and see what you can turn it into, by distorting it with the Arrow tool. Remember that the nature of the new curves depends on where you start to drag them from, and whether or not you hold down [Ctrl]. And remember Undo!

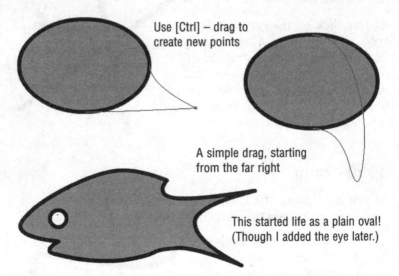

Use [Ctrl] – drag to create new points

A simple drag, starting from the far right

This started life as a plain oval! (Though I added the eye later.)

2.6 Using the Subselection tool

The Subselection tool displays and works with the anchor points. Though called *Sub*selection, this actually performs *super*selection – click anywhere on a compound object, such as a filled shape or crossed lines, and the whole thing is selected. (In contrast to the Selection tool which only selects the specific item that you click on.) The 'Sub' part of the name presumably refers to the fact that it uses the anchor points, which can be edited individually.

There are some significant differences in the ways that the Selection and Subselection tools work.

With the Subselection tool:

* You can select by clicking, or by dragging a rectangle over the object. You do not need to enclose the entire object. Once any part of a line is selected, the rest of that line *and any other lines which cross it* are also selected.

* You can only select lines – if you click on the fill nothing happens – but when you select the outline of a filled shape, the fill is then moved or distorted along with the outline.

* As soon as you touch a line, it is selected and can be edited immediately.

* You can only adjust a shape by moving the anchor points. If you drag on the line between the points, the whole selected drawing moves.

* You cannot bend a straight line with the Subselection tool.

* If an anchor point is at a junction, every line that meets at that junction will be affected if you move the point.

* When you drag on an anchor point on a curve, a line will appear on the curve, indicating the *tangent*. By dragging the *tangent handles* you can adjust the shape of the curve.

* For fine adjustment of an anchor point, click on it to select it, then use the arrow keys to nudge it a pixel at a time.

Practise!

1 If there is anything on the screen that you want to keep for later use, save it and start a new file. If not, use the Selection tool to select and erase the clutter from the stage.

2 Draw two crossed lines.

3 Click the **Subselection** tool.

4 Click anywhere on the length of a line. You should see blue dots appear at the end of each line and at the junction, joined by thin blue lines.

5 Drag on the line to move the shape without changing it.

6 Drag on the tip of a line and change its length and angle.

7 Click elsewhere on the stage to deselect the lines.

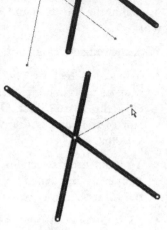

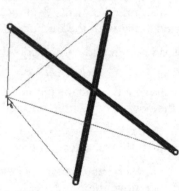

8 Click and drag on the anchor point at the centre to distort the cross.

9 Draw an oval elsewhere on the stage.

10 Using the Subselection tool, click on the oval to display its anchor points.

11 Drag an anchor point out to one side.

12 Drag on a tangent handle to adjust the curve leading up to the anchor point.

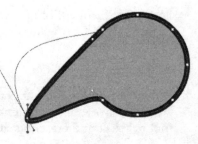

2.7 Selecting with the Lasso tool

The Lasso can be used to select an irregular area of the stage. You can define the area in two ways:

- Drag a freehand outline that more or less encloses the area – Flash will connect your start and end points with a straight line.

- Turn on the **Polygon** modifier in the **Options** area. You can then draw the outline as a series of straight lines. Click where you want each point and double-click at the end. Click the **Polygon** button again if you want to switch back to freehand.

- Use a mixture of straight lines and freehand – hold down [**Alt**] and click when you want to draw a straight line between two points. This is slower the drawing freehand but more accurate – use it when you need to make a precise outline.

An area selected with the Lasso can be moved, transformed (see section 2.8), copied or deleted. You can also redefine the colour or other aspects of the stroke or fill of the objects in the selection area. You cannot, obviously, edit individual lines within the selection.

The Magic Wand is used to select areas of the same or similar colour out of bitmap images.

Practise!

1 Use your newly-acquired line and circle drawing and editing skills to create an image of someone walking a dog (or whatever you fancy, this is just a suggestion!). The drawing should have at least two main components, and these should be too complex and too close together to be able to select either using the Arrow tool.

2 Select the **Lasso** tool.

3 Use freehand or [**Alt**] – click to enclose the dog (or another similar component of the drawing).

Drawing freehand is quicker, but it can be tricky to get the line exacly where you need it

With the Polygon modifier or the [Alt] – click method you get straight lines which can be positioned more accurately

4 *To move the selected area,* place the cursor anywhere over it – the cursor will

   have a 4-way arrow  – and drag the thin grey out- line into place.

5 *To redefine the stroke of the lines* in the area, use the Stroke options in the Properties panel (see pages 20–21).

6 *To copy the selected area,* use **Edit > Copy**, the **Copy** button or press [**Ctrl**] – [**C**].

7 *To delete the area,* press [**Delete**] or [**Backspace**].

2.8 Transformations

Transformations can, of course, be used for creating the original images at the start of the movie-making process, but they also have a very important part to play in animation. Take an object, rotate it through 180° after 10 frames, then through 180° again after another 10 frames, and you have the basis of a spinning object. Changing the size over time can give the illusion of movement towards or from the viewer; skewing can give the effect of 3-D rotation. We will look at these uses of transformations in Chapter 4 – let's master still drawing first.

You can transform any shape, but some do not show up too well on either lines or circles. Time for a new shape – a rectangle will do the job. Click 🔲 – if you find that you are offered a choice of Rectangle and Polystar tools, take the rectangle. We will look at the alternatives and options in the next chapter.

Drawn objects can be rotated or resized in two ways:

* Freehand, using the **Free Transform** tool
* By specifying exact values on the **Transform** panel.

Using the Free Transform tool

The tool has four modifiers. Select:

* **Rotate and skew** to rotate or skew a shape. *Skew* moves one side of the object or its bounding rectangle (the imaginary rectangle that encloses it), leaving the other side unchanged.

* **Scale** to change the size of a shape.

* **Distort** to change the shape by dragging one anchor point.

* **Envelope** to adjust the curvature of a shape.

The tool is used in the same general way for all modifiers.

1 Select the object with the **Free Transform** tool.

2 Click a modifier. Handles will appear at the corners and sides of the object or its bounding rectangle.

3 Drag on a handle – the effect depends upon the modifier and whether you drag on a corner or a side handle.

The Rotate modifier 🔁

* Corner handles rotate the shape around its pivot – this is initially in the centre but can be moved.

* A side handle moves that side only, and without changing the distance across the shape.

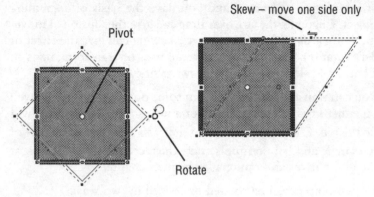

Skew – move one side only

Pivot

Rotate

The Scale modifier 🔳

* Corner handles enlarge or shrink the shape, while retaining the original proportions.

* A side handle changes the width or height.

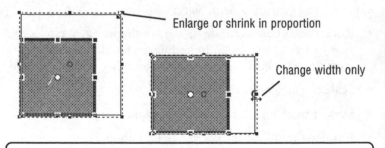

Enlarge or shrink in proportion

Change width only

Mirroring

If you want to mirror the drawing, there are Flip Vertical and Flip Horizontal commands on the Modify > Transform submenu. You can also use Free Transform for this. If you drag a side handle right across and out the other side of the drawing you will mirror it left to right or top to bottom.

The Distort modifier 🖉

* If you drag on a corner handle, that corner and its adjacent sides will be pulled in or out, while the opposite two sides stay fixed. The object will distort to fit the new shape

* If you drag on a side handle, the opposite side will stay fixed, but all the rest moves with the handle – it is like skewing and scaling at the same time.

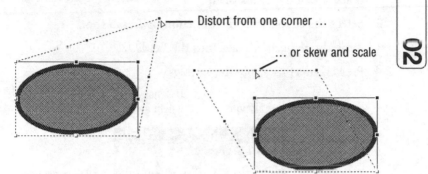

—— Distort from one corner ...

... or skew and scale

The Envelope modifier 🖻

This brings up the anchor points and puts tangent handles on every point. It's the same as using the Subselection tool except that all the tangent handles are present from the start, and stay visible for as long as you are working with the tool. If you are trying to make complex changes to the curves:

* Drag the anchor points to move them.

* Drag the tangent handles to change the curves either side of an anchor point.

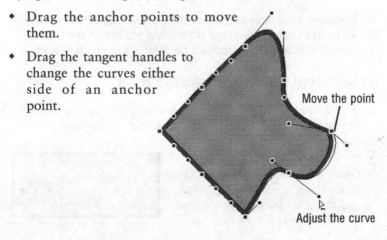

Move the point

Adjust the curve

The Transform panel

The options on the **Transform** panel allow you to be more precise when you are changing the width, height, angle and skew of an object.

To use the Transform panel:

1 Open the **Window** menu, point to **Design Panels** and click to place a tick by **Transform**.

2 Select the shape with the **Selection** or **Lasso** tool.

3 Type the required values into the fields.

4 Press **[Enter]** to apply the settings.

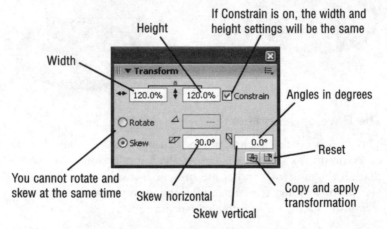

The **Transform** panel. Note the buttons in the bottom right. **Copy and apply transformation** creates a new copy of the shape and applies the transformation to both. **Reset** restores the drawing to its original shape.

Experiments with transformations

1 If you want to keep your movie for later use, save it and start a new file. If not, close the file and start a new one.

2 Click the **Rectangle** tool.

3 Click and drag to draw a rectangle in the middle of the stage – make it wider than it is high.

4 Use any of the selection tools to select the rectangle and its fill, then open the **Modify** menu and click **Group**. (This converts the sides and fill into a single unit which will be easier to handle and to animate.)

5 Bring **Transform** to the front of the Info panel – use **Window > Panels > Transform** if you can't see the panel.

6 Make sure that **Constrain** is off, and type 50% as the **width** then press [**Enter**]. The rectangle should become narrower and more square.

7 Click the **Reset** button to restore the original shape.

8 Set the **Rotate** angle to 45° and press [**Enter**].

9 Click the **Reset** button, then select the **Skew** radio button so that its fields become active. Enter 60° in the **Skew horizontal** field.

10 Reset and try 60° in the **Skew vertical** field.

11 See what happens if you skew both horizontally and vertically by the same – and by different – amounts.

A 60° horizontal (x) skew

A 60° vertical (y) skew

12 Now try the same kinds of transformations with the Free Transform tool and its modifiers. When would you use which method?

2.9 Colour

There are two approaches to setting colours in Flash:

* The colour controls in the Toolbox or in the Properties panel
* The Color Mixer and Swatches panels.

The first approach leads to versions of the Swatches panel.

The Toolbox and Properties colour controls

These are the simplest. You can set colours before you draw an object, or change the colour of a selected object.

1 Click on the colour sample to open a palette of swatches of predefined colours.

2 Click on a colour to select it.

3 If there are no suitable pre-defined colours, click the ● icon at the top right to open the standard colour dialog box. Define your colour in the usual way and click **OK** to apply it.

4 The palette for the Fill colour has an extra line with a small selection of gradient fills. You cannot redefine these from here.

In the Toolbox, there are also three extra options, to be found in the buttons below the Fill colour control:

* ▣ **Black/White** changes the colour to either black or white, whichever is the nearest.

* ☑ **Nil** set the Stroke or Fill to no colour. Use this before drawing with the Oval or Rectangle tool, to produce empty shapes or fills without outlines. It has no effect on existing objects.

   There is also a ☑ button on the palettes.

* 🔁 **Swap Colors** changes the stroke colour for the fill colour, and vice versa.

The Color Mixer panel

This is where you can define your own colours. There are also some advanced options that you will only find here.

To define a colour:

1 Click on the Stroke or Fill colour icon. (Not on the sample beside it – clicking that displays the swatches palette.)

2 Set the shade and brightness by clicking and dragging in the Colour bar, *or*

Set the RGB (Red, Green, Blue) values by typing them in, or by clicking on the arrows to the right and using the sliders.

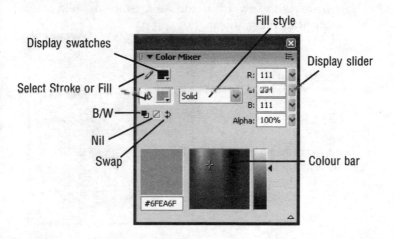

Fill style

Display swatches

Display slider

Select Stroke or Fill

B/W

Nil

Swap

Colour bar

Gradient fills

A Fill colour can be solid, a linear or radial gradient, or a bitmap – select the type from the drop-down list at the top of the tab.

A solid fill colour is set in the same way as the stroke colour. We'll come back to Bitmap fills when we look at graphics in Chapter 8. At this point let's concentrate on the gradient fills.

Linear and radial gradient fills are defined in the same way. The difference is how they are applied to the object: a radial gradient spreads from the centre, linear gradient changes from one side to the other. (And if you want the gradient to change at a different angle, use the Fill Transform tool later – see section 3.6.)

The coloured markers beneath the gradient display show the colours at either end – obviously – but also define where the gradient starts. Either or both can be moved inwards to create a band of solid colour before the gradient begins.

To define a gradient fill:

1 Select the type – radial or linear.

2 Click on the colour marker at one end.

3 Define the colour in the Colour bar, or click on the sample to open the swatches and select a predefined colour.

4 Repeat for the other colour marker.

5 Drag the markers inwards if you want bands of solid colour before or after the gradient.

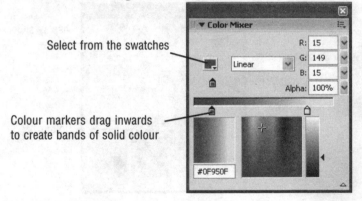

Select from the swatches

Colour markers drag inwards to create bands of solid colour

The Alpha value

Alpha refers to the density of the colour. When you are drawing on a single layer, a low value simply produces a paler colour. However, when you have several layers, if an object in a higher layer is given a low Alpha value, it becomes semi-transparent and objects in lower layers can be seen through it. (At 0, the colour disappears completely.)

There is also an Alpha effect which can be used in animation. We'll look at this in Chapter 5.

The Swatches panel

This display is essentially the same as the palettes that can be opened from the colour controls in the Toolbox. The only differences are that gradient fill icons are a little larger and easier to see and you cannot open the **Colour** dialog box from here.

◆ *To open the panel*, use **Window > Design Panels > Color Swatches**.

2.10 Overlapping

When you are drawing an object, or moving a selected object, it can pass freely over any existing objects without affecting them. However, when you release an object on top of another, it will replace whatever was underneath. If you move or delete the new object, there will be a hole. Done accidentally, this can be most annoying (though at least we have Undo), but done deliberately it can be a useful drawing technique. Try it and see.

1 Clear the stage.

2 Select the **Rectangle** tool. In the **Properties** panel, set the Stroke to 2 points, black and the Fill to solid red.

3 Draw a rectangle around 150 pixels wide by 40 high.

4 Use the **Free Transform** tool to skew the rectangle, tipping it about 30° to the right – it will be the body of a sports car! Add a windscreen if you like.

5 Select the **Oval** tool. Set the Stroke to 4 points.

6 Draw a circle aproximately 50 pixels across. We will use this to cut out the space for a wheel and leave a wheel arch.

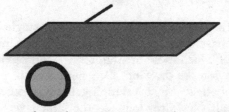

7 Select the circle and copy it – we need two wheels!

8 Drag one circle so that it overlaps the rectangle at the front.

9 Click on the outline of the circle and you will see that it has been split into two arcs where it crosses the rectangle.

10 Select the lower arc and the fill, and delete them both.

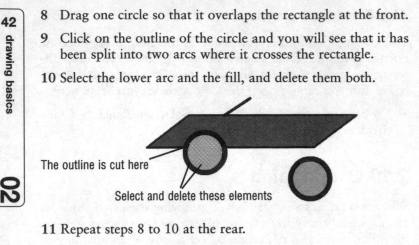

The outline is cut here

Select and delete these elements

11 Repeat steps 8 to 10 at the rear.

12 Draw a wheel – a circle about 45 pixels across with an 8 point stroke and a radial fill, will do the job.

13 Copy it and drag the two wheels into place.

14 Save the document. We'll animate this later.

2.11 Grouping

Grouping turns drawn lines and fills into a single object, and also fixes the basic definition of the image. This is important for animation – of which more in Chapter 4 – and can also be convenient when you are drawing. One big bonus is that grouped images are not affected by overlapping, in fact, you cannot draw over them at all. New drawings (on the same layer) will always go below the grouped object, and they are not overlapped by it either. Move the object, and the drawn image beneath will still be intact. Grouped images are simpler to manipulate – they can be selected with a single click and copied, moved and transformed more easily than is the case with a collection of lines and shapes.

To *group a drawing:*

1 Select the lines and shapes that make up the image.

2 Open the **Modify** menu and select **Group**. A thin blue line will appear around the object to show that it is selected.

The grouped object can be transformed as a whole, but if you need to change the shape, size or colour of any component part, you must first ungroup it.

| Modify | Text | Commands | Control | Window | Help |

Document...	Ctrl+J
Convert to Symbol...	F8
Break Apart	Ctrl+B
Bitmap	▶
Symbol	▶
Shape	▶
Timeline	▶
Timeline Effects	▶
Transform	▶
Arrange	▶
Align	▶
Group	Ctrl+G
Ungroup	Ctrl+Shift+G

To *ungroup an object:*

1 Select the object.

2 Open the **Modify** menu and select **Ungroup**.

2.12 Arranging the order

Though grouped images aren't changed by overlapping, they can still obscure or be obscured. Enter the **Arrange** options. These allow you to change the depth of grouped images in relation to each other.

To *change the order or appearance:*

1 Select the object that you want to rearrange.

2 Open the **Modify** menu, point to **Arrange,** and click on an option. You may need to use **Bring Forward** and **Send Backward** several times, as the overlapping ones may not be next to each other in the order of appearance.

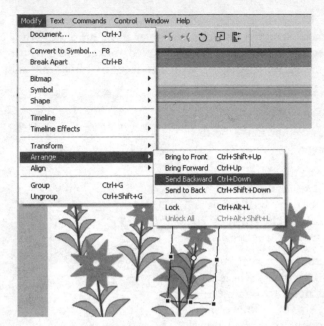

| Modify | Text | Commands | Control | Window | Help |

Document...	Ctrl+J
Convert to Symbol...	F8
Break Apart	Ctrl+B
Bitmap	▶
Symbol	▶
Shape	▶
Timeline	▶
Timeline Effects	▶
Transform	▶
Arrange	▶
Align	▶
Group	Ctrl+G
Ungroup	Ctrl+Shift+G

Bring to Front	Ctrl+Shift+Up
Bring Forward	Ctrl+Up
Send Backward	Ctrl+Down
Send to Back	Ctrl+Shift+Down
Lock	Ctrl+Alt+L
Unlock All	Ctrl+Alt+Shift+L

Grouped objects are easily duplicated and transformed – here one flower is rapidly becoming a flower bed, and the Arrange options let me push the little ones to the back to give some depth to the scene.

Exercises

1 Using mainly ovals, draw a cartoon cat, or other 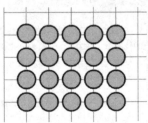 animal.

2 Use the guides and the grid to set up a 5 × 4 array of ovals, 40 pixels in diameter, 10 pixels apart.

   Hint: Edit the grid to a spacing of 50 × 50 pixels.

3 Fill the background of a stage with a rectangle containing a linear gradient that ranges from deep red at the top down to bright yellow at the bottom.

   Hint: The gradient will run left to right, so rotate the shape.

Summary

* A raster graphics image is defined by the colour and brightness of each pixel.

* A vector graphics image is the sum of its component lines and shapes, each of which is defined mathematically.

* The Line tool draws straight lines. These can be curved and modified later.

* The appearance of a line is defined by its stroke settings – style, thickness and colour.

* Edit > Undo allows you to undo your recent actions.

* You can position items accurately using one or more of the rules, the guides and the grid.

* Snap options can be turned on to simplify the alignment of objects with the guides, the grid and/or other objects.

* The Selection tool is used for selecting and modifying lines and shapes.

* The Subselection tool displays the anchor points of lines. These can be moved by dragging; curves can be reshaped using the tangent handles on the points.

* The Lasso tool allows you to select irregular shapes.

* Using the Free Transform tool or the Transform panel you can rotate, skew, scale, distort and envelope objects.

* Colours can be set with the Color Mixer panel or the Swatches.

* If drawn lines or shapes overlap, they become part of each other, replacing whatever drawing lays underneath.

* Grouping a drawing converts it to a single object. This cannot be edited without ungrouping. If grouped images overlap each other, you can change the order in which they lie on the stage.

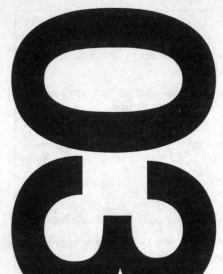

03
the drawing tools

In this chapter you will learn:

- how to use the Pen, Pencil, Brush and other tools
- how to set Rectangle and Polystar options
- how to transform gradient fills
- about the viewing tools

3.1 The Toolbox

We have dipped into the Toolbox several times already, so it really must be time that we had a proper look at it.

The Toolbox is the simplest way to access the drawing tools and their options, though the tools can also be selected by pressing the letter key shown after their names.

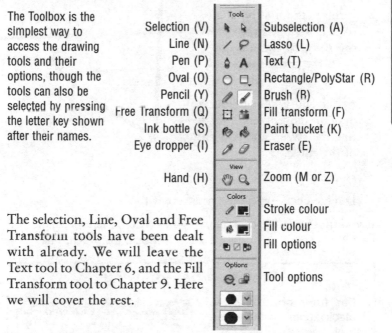

Selection (V)
Line (N)
Pen (P)
Oval (O)
Pencil (Y)
Free Transform (Q)
Ink bottle (S)
Eye dropper (I)

Hand (H)

Subselection (A)
Lasso (L)
Text (T)
Rectangle/PolyStar (R)
Brush (R)
Fill transform (F)
Paint bucket (K)
Eraser (E)

Zoom (M or Z)

Stroke colour
Fill colour
Fill options

Tool options

The selection, Line, Oval and Free Transform tools have been dealt with already. We will leave the Text tool to Chapter 6, and the Fill Transform tool to Chapter 9. Here we will cover the rest.

3.2 The Pen

This can be used for straight or curved lines – and to change existing lines from straight to curved, or vice versa. The Pen produces visible anchor points as it draws, with tangent handles at the end points of curves. Using this is similar to drawing with the Line tool, then editing it with the Subselection tool. In fact, it can be used with the Subselection tool for editing drawings.

This is a sophisticated tool, and needs some practice.

To draw straight lines:

1 Click where you want the line to start.

2 Click where the line is to end.

3 Repeat step 2 to draw another line running on from the last.

To draw curves:

1 Instead of clicking, hold down the mouse button on the corner – tangent handles will appear.

2 If this is the first point of a drawing, drag the tangent handle to set the initial path of the curve.

3 At the end point of a curve, drag the tangent handle to define the sweep and end path of the curve.

To stop drawing:

◆ Double-click, or choose a different tool.

If you finish exactly back where you started, then the shape will be filled, otherwise it will be a continuous, but open, line.

Precision pen-drawing

For finer control when placing points with the Pen tool, you can replace the pen cursor with a crosshair.

You can make this permanent by turning on Show Precise Cursors in the Editing tab of the Preferences dialog box (use Edit > Preferences... to open this), or switch between the pen and the crosshair cursor by pressing the [Caps Lock] key while you are drawing.

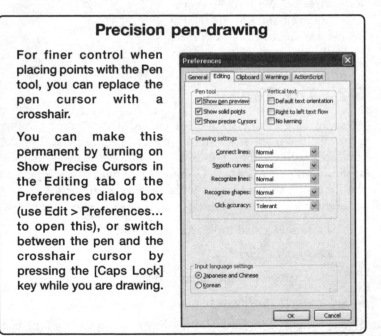

On an existing drawing (after selecting it with the Subselection tool), the Pen tool can be used in two ways:

- Click on a curve anchor point, and it will convert it to a corner point – and straighten the lines coming off from it.

- Click on a line to create a new corner point.

3.3 The Rectangle/PolyStar

Several of the tools have modifiers, but this is the only one with two distinct modes. If you click and hold on its Toolbox icon, the **Rectangle/PolyStar** menu will open. Click on the one you want. As well as selecting it, this will also set that mode as the default, and display the appropriate Toolbox icon.

The Round Rectangle modifier

The Rectangle tool has only one modifier – the round rectangle radius. This sets the roundness of the corners, measured in points.

Experimentation will show what is the best setting for the job in hand – and note that you cannot change the roundness of an existing rectangle.

To change the radius of the corners:

1 Click the Round Rectangle Radius modifier 🖝.

2 Set the radius and click **OK**.

3 Draw the rectangle. How does it look? Do you need to Undo and start again?

The PolyStar tool

Did I say two distinct modes? Perhaps that should have been three. The PolyStar mode of this tool can draw either polygons or stars. Both shapes can have from 3 to 32 points, and you can also set the sharpness of the star points.

To draw a star or polygon:

1 Select the **PolyStar** tool.

2 In the **Properties** area, set the stroke and fill colours, then click the Options... button.

3 At the **Tool Settings** dialog box, select the **Style** (*star* or *polygon*).

4 Enter the **Number of Sides**.

5 For stars, set the **Star point size**.

6 Click **OK**.

7 Click in the centre of where the shape will appear and drag outwards to set the size.

8 Drag to rotate the shape to the desired angle.

9 Release the mouse button.

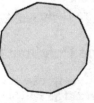

Star point sizes

0.1   0.5   1.0 (maximum)

Some polygons

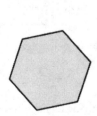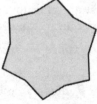

3 = triangle   6 = hexagon   12 = duodecagon

3.4 The Pencil

Most of us find it hard to draw smooth lines on a computer but Flash has the solution – it automatically tidies up your freehand drawing. There are three **pencil modes**, offering a different degree of tidying:

- **Straighten** makes lines straight or turns them into simple curves – a complex line may be straightened in segments.

- **Smooth** turns lines into flowing curves.

- **Ink** just takes off the rougher edges.

| Straighten | Smooth | Ink |

The sun shining on a tree (?!?!), drawn in three pencil modes.

To draw with the Pencil:

1 Select the **Pencil** tool.

2 In the **Options** area, click the **Pencil mode** button and select a mode – only use **Straighten** if you really want straight lines.

3 In the **Properties** panel, set the colour and define the stroke.

4 Draw! When you release the mouse, the line will be tidied up.

3.5 The Brush

The Brush paints in the current fill colour – solid, gradient or bitmap. It has four options, and we'll start with the simplest.

Brush size and shape

These define the brush. Drop down the lists to select the size and shape – and note that the size is always shown as a circle, whever the shape.

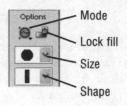
Mode
Lock fill
Size
Shape

Paint modes

There are five modes which control where the paint goes.

*   **Normal**: covers anything it goes over.
*   **Fills**: paints only fills and background, but not any lines.
*   **Behind**: paints only the background.
*   **Selection**: paints only selected objects.
*   **Inside**: paints the fill of an object, wiping up any stray brushmarks that go beyond it. This will only correct minor errors – if you splash paint all over the place, it won't work. It can also distort the outer line, so use carefully.

Options

Paint Normal
Paint Fills
Paint Behind
Paint Selection
✓ Paint Inside

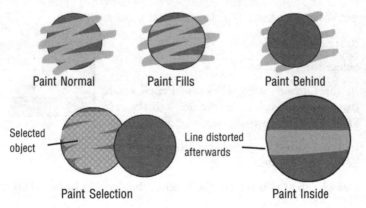

Paint Normal   Paint Fills   Paint Behind

Selected object   Line distorted afterwards

Paint Selection   Paint Inside

Lock Fill

This can only be used with gradient and bitmap fills. Normally with these, the fill is centred in each object, wherever it may be on the stage. With Lock Fill active, the fill pattern extends over the whole stage and is centred on the first object that is painted.

On – gradient spread across stage

Off – each object filled with separate gradient

The same gradient fill applied with Lock Fill on and off. Lock Fill works best with bitmaps (see Chapter 8) or with tight gradients.

3.6 The Paint bucket

This can be used for recolouring fills. There are two options:

* **Lock Fill** is the same as the Brush option.

* **Gap** size relates to any gaps in the enclosing lines. The bucket can be set to ignore gaps of varying sizes, filling the shape up to where the line should be. The fill will only flood out through a gap if there is the same fill colour the other side of the gap.

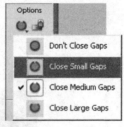

Options

Don't Close Gaps

Close Small Gaps

✓ Close Medium Gaps

Close Large Gaps

Painting by the bucketful. To recolour several fills at once, select them all before selecting the bucket. Pour into any one and they will all be refilled.

Off-centre radial gradients

If you want an off-centre radial gradient fill, click the Paint bucket where you want the centre of the gradient to be.

3.7 The Fill transform tool

A simple linear gradient runs from left to right across the object; a simple radial gradient spreads at the same rate in all directions. The Fill Transform tool allows you to change the angle and rate of change of both types.

1 Select the **Fill Transform** tool.

2 Click on the fill.

3 Drag the central handle to move the centre of the pattern.

To transform a linear gradient fill:

4 Drag the square handle in or out to change the rate of the gradient.

5 Drag the round handle to rotate the fill pattern.

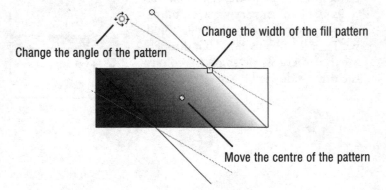

Change the width of the fill pattern

Change the angle of the pattern

Move the centre of the pattern

To transform a radial gradient fill:

6 Drag the middle of the three handles in or out to change the rate of the gradient.

7 Drag the square handle to make the oval flatter or rounder.

8 Drag the outer round handle to rotate the pattern.

Bitmap fills can also be transform with this tool (see Chapter 8).

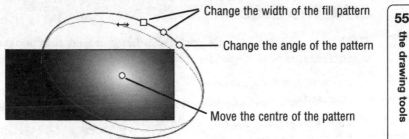

Change the width of the fill pattern

Change the angle of the pattern

Move the centre of the pattern

3.8 The Ink bottle

This is used for recolouring or reformatting lines. You could produce the same results by selecting the lines and changing their settings in the Properties panels, but the Ink bottle approach is probably more efficient where you want to change a lot of lines to the same new definition.

To use the Ink bottle:

1 Select the Ink bottle tool.

2 In the **Properties** area, define the stroke and the colour.

3 Click on a line to reformat it. If the line meets or crosses another, it will be reformatted up to the junction only.

4 Repeat to format other lines.

3.9 The Eyedropper

This is used along with the Paint bucket or Ink bottle, for copying fill and stroke colours.

To use the Eyedropper:

1 Select the **Eyedropper** tool.

2 Click on a line or a fill area.

3 If you click on a line, its colour and stroke will be picked up. The cursor will change to the Ink bottle and the line format can then be applied to other lines.

4 If you click a fill, the cursor will change to the Paint bucket and the colour and pattern can then be applied to other fills.

3.10 The Eraser

The Eraser rubs out lines and/or fills. What is erased, and under what circumstances, depends upon the mode.

Faucet

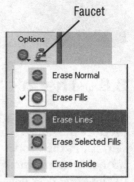

* **Normal:** anything crossed by the eraser is erased.

* **Fills:** fills are erased, but the lines are left.

* **Lines:** leaves the fills intact.

* **Selected Fills:** erases only fills and only of selected objects.

* **Inside:** erases only the fill of a shape, and you must start to erase within it.

The Faucet

This modifier makes the eraser work like the Ink bottle or the Paint brush. Clicking on a line or fill will erase it – or at least, will erase as much as would have been selected if you clicked it with the Selection tool.

* Click the Faucet to turn it on or off – the cursor gives a clear indication of the mode.

Eraser shape and size

The Eraser can be round or square and of a range of sizes.

With the smaller sizes, erasing lines may not appear to work. This is because the stroke extends out beyond the defined line, so although erasing may cause a break in the line, the rounding at the ends of the new segments may merge to give the illusion of a continuous line.

The Eraser breaks the line, but if the eraser size is less than twice the line thickness, the gap is filled by the rounding either side of the break.

3.11 The viewing tools

Zoom

Using the Zoom tool is one of three ways in which you can zoom in on your work to draw and check details.

To zoom in and out:

1 Select the **Zoom** tool.

2 In the Options area, select the **Enlarge** or **Reduce** modifier, as required.

3 Click where you want the centre of the display to be after zooming.

4 Click again to move further in or out.

♦ When using Zoom you can hold [**Alt**] to switch from Enlarge to Reverse or vice versa.

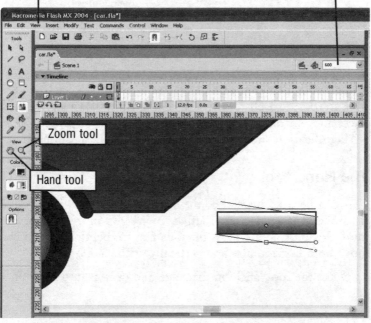

The closer you get to an object, the more accurate adjustments you can make. Here I'm tweaking the gradient fill on a small component.

The View menu

You can also change the zoom level through the **View** menu.

*   The **Zoom In** and **Zoom Out** commands are the same as using the Zoom tool, except that you cannot set the centre for the display.

*   The **Magnification** submenu offers a range of Zoom levels.

After you have zoomed in, use the scroll bars or the Hand tool (see below) to move to the part of the display that you want to examine.

Note the [Ctrl] keystrokes – these are handy if you want to flick quickly between very close, to set details, and back out, to see the overall effect

The Zoom field

This third approach to zooming is the most flexible. You can select a level from the drop-down list (the same as on the **Zoom > Magnification** submenu) or type your specific requirements.

The Hand tool

This can be used instead of the scroll bars for moving around the stage. It is a better alternative, giving you more control and more flexibility – the most obvious feature being that you can move both horizontally and vertically at the same time.

*   Select the tool, click on the stage and drag it into position.

Exercises

1 Using any combination of tools, draw a townscape background for a movie. Save it – you could build on this later.

2 Create a night sky background. Hint: for sharply-pointed stars, set the stroke to Nil.

3 Draw a circle with a radial fill, and transform the fill to give the illusion of a sphere.

4 Explore the effect of turning Lock Fill on and off by drawing a set of shapes with the same gradient fill.

Summary

♦ There is a comprehensive set of tools in the Toolbox for drawing and modifying lines and shapes.

♦ The Pen can draw or modify lines, and can produce complex curves – but it needs practice.

♦ The Rectangle and PolyStar tools are accessed from the same button.

♦ When you are drawing with the Pencil, the system can smooth or straighten the lines for you.

♦ The Brush and the Paint bucket can create or change fill colours.

♦ The Fill transform tool allows you to customize gradient and bitmap fills.

♦ The Ink bottle is used for recolouring lines.

♦ Use the Eyedropper tool to copy existing colours.

♦ The Erase can be used to remove lines or fills or both.

♦ Use the Zoom tool to get close to your work, and the Hand tool to move the stage within the Flash window.

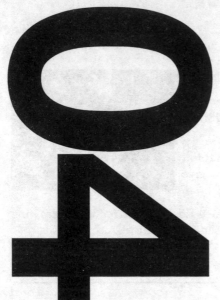

04

tweens and the timeline

In this chapter you will learn:

- about the Timeline
- how to create motion tweens
- about onion skins
- how to control frames and keyframes
- about shape tweening

4.1 The Timeline

This is where animation is produced and controlled. Let's look at what's there.

Below the number line are one or more *layer* lines. A layer can be thought of as a transparent sheet on which drawings can be made, with each layer capable of being animated at its own pace and in its own way. (We'll get to layers in Chapter 5.)

The layer lines are divided into *frames*, each one representing a moment in time during the movie – which typically run at 12 frames per second. When you select a frame on the Timeline, you will see what will appear on the stage at that moment.

There are two types of frame: a *keyframe* is one where you can create or modify a drawing. The ordinary frames between are controlled by Flash. If there is no animation, they will show whatever was in the previous keyframe, otherwise they will show a 'tween'. A keyframe is indicated by a dot – black if there is a drawing in the frame, empty if the stage is blank at that point.

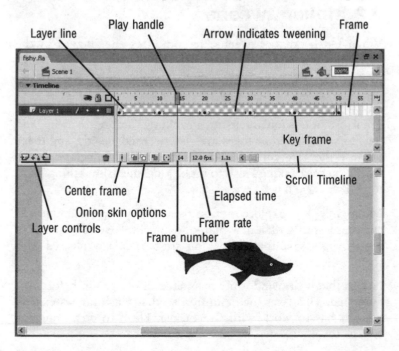

Tweens are images produced by Flash to show the transitional stages as an object moves or changes shape, size or colour from its state in one keyframe to its state in the next.

The *play handle* – the red guideline with a rectangle at the top – allows you to move backwards and forwards through the frames

There are several sets of controls in the bar at the bottom of the Timeline area:

- On the far left are three controls used when working with layers. We'll come back to them in the next chapter.

- *Center frame* is useful when your movies get longer. This scrolls the Timeline so that the current frame is in the centre.

- The *Onion skin options* are ways of looking at several frames at once. We will get to those shortly.

- The frame and time displays show exactly where you are at. They can be handy for fine-tuning your timings.

4.2 Motion tweens

When Flash creates tweens, it compares the images in the keyframes at the start and end, works out how the vectors change then divides the change values by the number of frames, redrawing the images between accordingly. If the change is movement, the tweening process is very simple and the results are perfect. Transformations (enlargement, shrinking, rotation, skewing and the like) and colour changes are also tweened exactly, and that's because they are controlled by mathematical calculations. It's when you start asking Flash to make judgements that things tend to go awry. We'll get back to this.

Meanwhile, let's explore motion tweens. Try these examples. In each case, start with a new blank document. Save at least one of the movies – save them all if you are particularly pleased with them!

Notice that a drawing is always made into a group before it is animated. This fixes the definition so that Flash knows exactly what it has to work with. If you ask Flash to create motion tweens for ungrouped images, the results can be unpredictable.

Simple motion

1 Create a small object on one side of the screen and group it.

2 Click on frame 10 (or later) in the object's layer in the Timeline, and press [F6] to turn this into a keyframe.

3 Drag the object across the screen.

4 Right-click on any frame between the keyframes in the object's layer and select **Create Motion Tween**.

5 Use **Control > Rewind,** then **Control > Play** to see the animation.

I've animated a bullet (a rectangle with the front curved outwards).

Move, transform and rotate

1 Create a small object on the top of the stage. As we are going to rotate this, it mustn't be too regular – stick a blob or a line on one corner. Group it!

2 Click on frame 10 in the object's layer in the Timeline.

3 Drag the object down the stage, and use the **Free Transform** tool to enlarge it and rotate it through a half-circle (or thereabouts).

4 Right-click on a frame between the keyframes and select **Create Motion Tween**.

5 Use the **Control** menu options, or the play handle, to test the animation.

Tweening in the Properties panel

1 Create a small object at one edge of the stage. This is also going to be rotated, so make sure it visibly has a right way up. (I drew this head.) Group it!

2 Click on frame 10 in the object's layer in the Timeline.

3 Drag the object to the opposite side of the stage.

4 *Left*-click on a frame between the keyframes.

5 The **Properties** panel will now show the properties of the selected frame. In the central section, drop down the **Tween** list and select **Motion**.

6 In the **Rotate** options, select **CW** (ClockWise) and set the number of times you want it to rotate.

7 Play your movie.

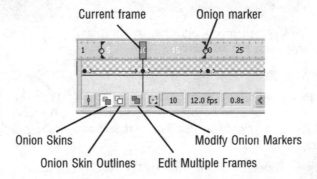

Motion tweens can be created from the **Properties** panel. The display changes to show these options after Motion has been selected.

4.3 Onion skins

You will have noticed in the last couple of pages that the motion screenshots show the start and end images, and outlines of the tweens. You are looking at 'onion skins' – faint or outline images of the tweened frames – which can be a very good way of checking the rate and flow of movement or transformation.

Onion skins come in two varieties and can be displayed in three ways. The controls are all in the bar below the layers.

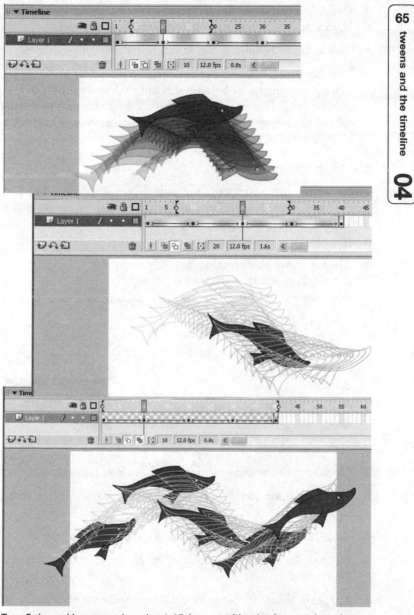

Top: Onions skins, spanning about 15 frames with a keyframe selected.
Middle: Onion skin outlines, again with a keyframe selected.
Bottom: Edit Multiple Frames turned on with outlines.

- **Onion Skins** show faint images of the tweens, and if a keyframe is selected, its contents are shown in full.

- **Onion Skin Outlines** is the same, but show only outlines.

- **Edit Multiple Frames** shows several keyframes at once, allowing any image to be edited. Onion skins or outlines can also be turned on at the same time. This combination is useful for fine-tuning movement as you can see how a keyframe change affects the whole path.

Onion markers

These set the boundaries for the onion skin displays. They can be changed by dragging them along the Timeline, or by using the **Modify Onion Markers** options.

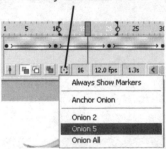

Modify Onion Markers

- **Always Show Markers** displays the markers whether the onion skins are on or not.

- **Anchor Onion** fixes the position of the onion skinning – if you move the play handle out of that area, no skins are shown.

- **Onion 2/5/All** set how many skins to display either side of the current frame.

To see onion skins:

1 Open one of the movies that you have just created.

2 Turn on **Onion Skins** and move the play handle to see them in action.

3 Turn on **Onion Skin Outlines** and **Edit Multiple Frames**.

4 Extend the markers to enclose both the start and the end keyframes.

5 Move the image in the start keyframe and note the change in the onion skin sequence.

4.4 Controlling frames and keyframes

Frames and keyframes can be inserted, deleted and converted from one to the other at any point. You can also drag single frames or sets along the Timeline. Flash recalculates the tweens immediately to reflect your alterations. The next exercise gives practice in these techniques.

1 You need to start with a simple animation showing movement across the stage between two points, around 10 frames apart. Use an existing movie or create a new one now – it should only take a moment or two.

2 Turn on **Onion Skin Outlines** and **Edit Multiple Frames** so that we can see what's going on.

3 Click on the end keyframe to select it. Now click on it again and drag it across to frame 20 or thereabouts.

Notice that you must click to select and then drag. Click and drag in one operation will not work here.

4 Select a frame mid-way through the movie and press [F6] to turn this into a keyframe. Drag the animated object up. The onion skins should show you that the path has changed.

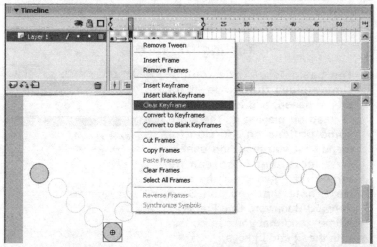

Plain frames and keyframes can be inserted or removed from the right-click menu. **Clear Keyframe** converts a keyframe to a plain one. Note that you can also cut, copy and paste frames (and their contents).

5 Insert new keyframes at the quarter and three-quarter points, moving the object down in these.

6 Play the movie to see how it looks.

7 Right-click on one of the new keyframes and select **Clear Keyframe** from the menu. What happens?

Inserting and removing frames

If you want to speed up or slow down an animation, you can insert or remove frames between the keyframes – the tweening will be automatically adjusted.

To *remove frames*:

1 Drag to select as many frames as you want to remove, from anywhere between the keyframes.

2 Right-click and select **Remove Frames** from the menu.

To *insert frames*:

1 Decide how many frames you want to insert. Drag to select that many from anywhere between the keyframes.

2 Right-click and select **Insert Frames** from the menu. The new frames will be slotted in next to the selected ones.

Testing the movie

The basic Test Movie routine simply plays the movie at its proper speed, and loops around to keep on playing it. There are some options on the Control menu that you may find useful. First, note that Loop can be turned off – just clear the tick. Next, note that you can Step Forward/Backward One Frame at a time – and that you can do this with the [.] and [,] keys.

Control	Debug	Window	Help
Play			Enter
Rewind			Ctrl+Alt+R
Test Project			Ctrl+Alt+P
Loop			
Step Forward One Frame			.
Step Backward One Frame			,
Set Breakpoint			
Remove Breakpoint			
Remove All Breakpoints			Ctrl+Shift+A
Continue			F10
Stop Debugging			F11
Step In			F6
Step Over			F7
Step Out			F8
Disable Keyboard Shortcuts			

4.5 The Ease factor

This has nothing to do with comfy chairs. The Ease factor is the relative speed of movement over time. The default is to spread the change of position equally over all the tweens, giving smooth movement, but you can set it to increase or decrease through the set of tweens.

* A negative Ease value produces acceleration.

* A positive Ease value produces deceleration.

Ease = –100

Closer tweens = slower

Ease = +100

To set the Ease factor:

1   Click on a tween frame, so that its properties are displayed.

2   In the Properties panel, type or use the slider to set the Ease value in the range –100 to +100.

3   Play the movie so that you can see the effect.

4.6 Shape tweens

When it comes to morphing – changing one shape to another – tweening has its limitations. Flash does some things well. It will morph a circle into a star, or a square into an oval then back to a square or on into any regular shape, just as smoothly as you like. And it can do this for a whole bunch of them at the same time. The problems come when you want to morph irregular shapes. But first, let's get Flash to show us what it can do.

• **When shape tweening, do not group the object. Flash needs it to be flexible.**

1 Start a new document – we want a clean stage and Timeline.

2 Draw a circle 100 pixels across in frame 1. Do not group it!

3 Make frame 20 a keyframe. The circle will have been copied into it. Delete it.

4 Use the PolyStar tool to create a star of a similar size. It can be in the same place as the circle if you like.

5 Select one of the frames in between.

6 In the **Properties** panel, select **Shape** in the **Tween** field.

7 Use the play handle to step slowly through the movie so that you can see the effect.

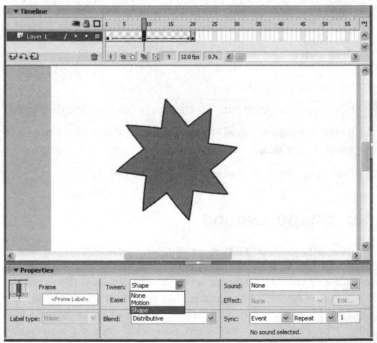

A shape tween, mid-way from a circle to an 8-point star. The Ease factor applies to shapes also.

Explore!

Working through the same steps as in the last exercise, try the following shape-changing animations:

* 1 large circle into 6 separate stars
* 6 small circles into 6 overlapping stars
* 1 large 8-pointed star into 8 5-pointed stars
* 1 large 8-pointed star into 5 small 8-pointed stars
* 4 rectangles and 3 5-sided polygons into 3 circles.

Which work best? What happens when the number of objects is different at the end? How far can you predict how the tweens will look, or where they will move as they are changing? Some of the transformations can be unexpectedly beautiful – have you found any that may be worth exploring further?

Colour changes

You can change the colour of objects while they are changing shape. Set the new colours in the end keyframe and Flash will smoothly adjust the colours in the tween images. This will not work with motion tweens as a grouped object cannot be redefined. However, you can use the Shape Tween routine (where the objects do not have to be grouped) to create motion – just move the object to a new position in the end keyframe.

Irregular shapes

Tweening regular shapes has its limitations, but with irregular shapes, the results are even more unpredictable once you get beyond very simple drawings. Try it and you will see.

1 Start a new document.

2 Draw a simple stick person – straight arms and legs, with no features – in frame 1.

3 Create a keyframe a little further along.

4 Move the whole person forward a little, then change the angles of his legs and arms a half stride. Try not to let a limb cross another – it will create a junction and give you a bend where you probably don't want one!

5 Use the Properties panel to set up shape tweens between the two keyframes.

6 Work through the movie with the play handle. How are the tweens?

You will need this movie for the next exercise. Save it, or leave it open and read on.

Shape hints

The problem is that Flash does not see the drawing as you do. It can only move anchor points and try to join them up appropriately. New to this version of Flash are *shape hints*. These are supposed to help Flash to tween more effectively. Well, they can sometimes help a bit, but they also have their limitations. We can use your stick man to test them out.

The theory behind shape hints is this. You place a hint – a small red circle labelled 'a' (then 'b', 'c', etc.) at a significant point on the drawing in the first keyframe, and a matching one on the equivalent point in the next keyframe.

Up to half a dozen or so more hints can be placed – Flash cannot cope with any more than this – at other crucial points on the drawing. For best results, the hints should be placed counter-clockwise, starting at the top left.

You can place the hints one at a time, flicking backwards and forwards between the keyframes, but in practice it is simplest to place all the hints on the first keyframe, then sort out the last keyframe. When you switch to it, all the hints will be there, but piled up in the centre, with the last on top. Drag them into place one by one. You will know when a hint is in place as Flash will turn it green (the one on the first frame will be turned yellow).

Let's give them a try.

1 Start from your stick person movie. Go to frame 1.

2 Open the **Modify** menu, point to **Shape** and select **Add Shape Hint**. It's a slow business placing hints by using the menu, so use the keyboard shortcut: **[Ctrl] – [Shift] – [H]**.

3 Drag the hint into place. Choose the end of a line, or a vertex, or the tip of a curve, and this first one should be the one closest to the top left of the drawing.

4 Add up to 5 more hints, working counter-clockwise round the drawing, as far as possible.

◆ If you want to remove a hint, do not press [Delete] – you will probably delete what's beneath it. Right-click on the hint and select **Remove Hint** from the menu. Notice that you can remove all the hints from here if you like.

Add Hint
Remove Hint
Remove All Hints
✔ Show Hints

5 Switch to the end keyframe. You should see the last hint in the middle of the drawing. Drag it into place – it's there when it turns green.

6 Moving the hint will have revealed another beneath. Keep dragging them into place until you reach the bottom of the pile.

7 Play the movie and see if the hints have helped to keep it together.

(1)   (2)   (3)   (4)

My hints didn't work quite as I had hoped. Here you can see the start (1) and end (3) keyframes, and one of the tweens (2) – I don't know where the head went! It's no better without hints. (4) is an unhinted tween.

It can be done!!

Don't let all these negatives get to you. It's important to understand the limitations of the system so that you do not get frustrated trying to make it do what it cannot. Smooth, slick animation is possible with Flash, and not that hard to achieve. But you must work with the system. Tweening fails if you try to make it do too much in a single layer – so the answer is to use more layers, as you will see in Chapter 5.

Exercises

1 Animate a polygon drawing so that it rolls in three or five zig-zags down the stage from the top left to the bottom right.

2 Use shape tweening to animate a red circle into a blue square and then into a larger yellow star over 40 frames.

3 Create an animation of a candle. Use shape hints to make it burn down smoothly.

Summary

+ The Timeline is where animation is processed and controlled.

+ The are two types of frame: keyframes contain your drawings; ordinary frames are controlled by Flash.

+ Motion tweens can be used to animate the movement or transformation of grouped objects.

+ By turning on onion skins, you can see a series of frames all at once.

+ Frames and keyframes can be moved, deleted or converted into each other.

+ The Ease factor can be set to make movement speed up or slow down over time.

+ Shape tweens can animate changes of shape. Sometimes shape hints can help to make the animation smoother.

05

layers

In this chapter you will learn:

- how to create and control layers
- about layers and animation
- how to use motion guides
- about mask layers
- how to set up Timeline effects
- about the Distribute to layers command

5.1 Working with layers

A layer is the Flash equivalent of a 'cel' – a transparent celluloid sheet – used in traditional hand-drawn animation. It can hold part of the total display, and this can be animated in its own way and at its own time. What you draw on one layer does not affect anything drawn on lower layers – it will obscure it at the time, but when you move the new drawing, the lower layer drawings will still be intact.

A very simple movie might have one layer for the background and one for the animated object, but there's nothing to stop you from having a background, foreground (and umpteen levels of middle ground) with a multiplicity of objects moving and transforming in front of, behind and between the scenery. Layers can also be used to hold sound files, ActionScript code and other non-drawn items.

The layer controls and tools can all be found on the left of the Timeline.

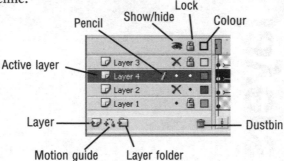

- **Show/hide** – layers can be hidden, which can make it easier to edit other layers.

- **Lock** – layers can be locked to protect them from accidental damage.

- **Colour** – the colour used for outlines when drawing is different for each layer, to remind you which layer you are on. Click once on this and the objects on the layer will only be shown as outlines. This can sometimes be useful.

- The **active layer** is highlighted, and contains the **pencil** icon. This will be crossed through if the layer is locked.

- Click the **Layer** button to create a new layer.

- The **Motion guide** button creates a layer to act as a motion guide (see section 5.3).

- If you have a lot of layers, click the **Layer folder** button and organise them into sets.

- You can drag unwanted layers to the **Dustbin** to delete them.

You will find the commands for all of these in the context menu that opens when you right-click on a layer.

Layer properties

If you want to check or change the outline colour or other properties of a layer, you can do this through the **Layer Properties** dialog box.

To open this, double-click on the colour block on the layer control bar.

Most of the properties can be changed directly on the layer control bar, as you will see later in this chapter.

Drawing and editing on layers

If you have layers, you need to take more care when drawing. As long as you ensure that the right layer has been highlighted before you start, drawing the initial shape or line is no different from doing it on a single layer.

The problems arise when you try to edit a drawing, because the selection tools can reach through the layers. If you drag a rectangle to select a shape on the active layer, you will in fact select every visible thing within the rectangle – on every layer.

(I didn't want the background!)

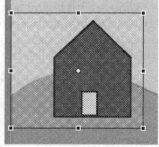

You can select the objects on a layer by selecting the layer. This can be useful if you want to do something with all of them – move, delete, recolour or turn them into a group. But it's not much help if you only want to select part of the drawing, and that is often the case when you are creating an image.

(I just want to move the chimney!)

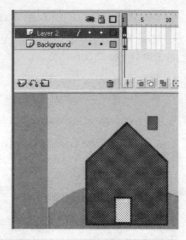

Hiding layers

One solution is to hide all the layers, except the one that you are working on.

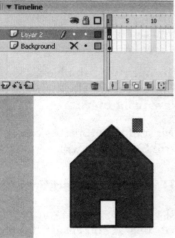

* Click in the column below the eye 🐵 to hide a layer.

* Click to remove the cross to show the layer again.

With the background hidden, it's easy to select part of the drawing on this layer.

Locking layers

A problem with hiding layers is that you often need to see other layers when you are working on a new object, so that you can draw it the right size and in the right place. When a layer is locked, you cannot select or edit any object drawn on it.

* Click in the column below the lock icon to lock a layer.

The layer can be unlocked later, if further work is needed.

Layer names

Layers are initially identified as Layer 1, Layer 2, etc. These can be replaced by meaningful names, and should be replaced if you have more than a few layers as you soon lose track of what is on which layer.

To rename a layer:

1 Double-click on the layer name in the Timeline. It will be highlighted.

2 Type a name that will remind you of what's on the layer.

5.2 Layered animation

Time to try this for yourself. In the following exercise, the design and images are suggestions only. The important thing is that your movie should have at least three layers holding a background, a foreground and a moving object. The background will stay still, the foreground will move across to the right to give the impression that the viewer is moving in relation to the scene, and the object will move across to the left – at a different rate and starting and ending at a different time. One of the points of this exercise is to demonstrate the independence of layers.

1 Start a new document.

2 In Layer 1, draw a background. I used a green rectangle at the bottom and a blue one at the top, then curved the lines in between to create 'hills'.

3 Double-click in the layer's name and change it to 'Background'. Click in the 🔒 Lock column and lock the layer.

4 Click 🔲 the Layer button to create a new layer. Draw a suitable foreground image here, on the left of the stage. I've used a tree, but it could be a building, a lamp post or anything you like. Group the finished drawing so that it can be motion tweened easily. (This will also protect it from damage while you are working on other layers.) Rename the layer.

A four layer animation. At this point the starting size and position of the
moving object is being adjusted.

5 If you like, create a middle ground layer containing distant
   scenery – I've done one with a set of houses. When working
   on this, you may find it helps to lock or hide the foreground.
   Group the drawing and rename the layer.

6 Create a final layer to hold the main moving object – in my
   case, it's an aeroplane (use your imagination). Group the
   drawing and rename the layer.

7 The layers are in the wrong order. The layer with the plane
   (or whatever) should be behind the foreground. Click on this
   layer in the Timeline and drag it down – you will see a thick
   grey line. Drop it below the foreground layer.

8 If you have a middle ground layer, move this below the plane.

9 Time to animate. Click into the foreground layer at around
   frame 30 and convert this to a keyframe. Drag the foreground
   image across to the right, and create motion tweens between.

- ◆ Now for the plane. The idea here is that this should come onto the stage slightly after the start of the movie, fly across and off the other side, leaving before the end.

10 Switch to the plane layer. Move the plane off the right edge. Create a keyframe at frame 20 and move the plane off the left edge there. Create motion tweens between the two.

11 The plane is flying too soon. Drag across from frames 1 to 20 in the plane layer to select them. Click into the middle of the set and drag it 5 frames to the right.

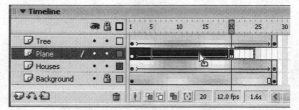

Blocks of frames can be moved to change the timing

12 If you have a middle ground layer, animate it. The movement should be in the same direction as the foreground, but slower.

13 Step through the movie with the play handle to check it. Are the layers in the right order to give the sense of perspective?

14 Play the movie to see it in real time. What do you think? Too fast isn't it. Let's insert some frames.

15 Starting at frame 10 in the top layer, drag down and across to frame 20 in the bottom to select 10 frames in each layer. Right-click and select **Insert Frames** from the menu. That will slow down the action a bit.

5.3 Motion guides

The normal motion tweening takes the objects on a straight line from their start to end points. If you want an object to take a more complex route, you can either set up a series of keyframes, one at each turn in the road, or you can use a motion guide. This is a path, drawn on a linked layer. The object is snapped onto the path at the start and end points, in the start and end keyframes, and Flash produces tweens which follow the path.

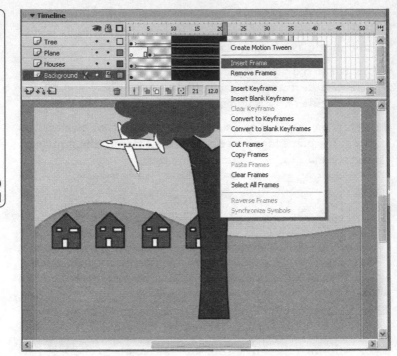

Inserting frames to slow down the movie. You can insert frames or remove them from individual layers to adjust their speed without affecting the rest.

A couple of points to note before you start:

* The motion path can be drawn with the Pen, Pencil or Line tools – or any combination of them – and can be bent or curved however you like. What is important is that the path must form a continuous line, and it must not cross itself.

* Any number of objects can be attached to the same motion guide. For best results, each object should be on its own layer. Create a new layer or drag an existing one to just beneath the motion guide to link to its path.

* You can have any number of different motion guides, if you want to move objects along different paths.

* The object can made to keep the same angle in relation to the path – so it will tilt as it goes round.

1 Start a new document.

2 Draw a suitable object for animating over a winding path. I'm using a flying brick. You can use your own imagination. We are going to use motion tweens, so group the object.

3 Create an end keyframe at frame 40.

4 Right-click between the keyframes and select **Create Motion Tween**.

5 In the **Properties** pane, check that **Snap** is turned on. The **Orient to path** option can be on or off as you like – try first with it on.

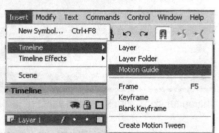

6 Open the **Insert** menu, point to **Timeline** and select **Motion Guide**, or right-click on the layer and select **Add Motion Guide**.

7 Use the **Pencil**, **Pen** or **Line** tool to draw a line that wanders over the screen – without crossing itself.

8 Go to frame 1 and position the object over the start of the path. If you point to the centre of the object, you should see a small circle in the outline when you move it. This will turn into a larger, darker circle when it is exactly over the line.

9 Go to the end frame and locate the object at the end of the line.

10 Use the play handle or **Control > Play** to see the animation.

11 Turn off the visibility of the motion guide layer.

12 Use **Control > Test Movie** to see the finished result.

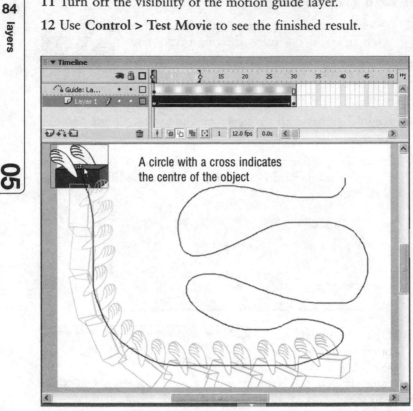

A circle with a cross indicates
the centre of the object

The onion skins here show the effect of turning on **Orient to path**.

No luck?

If your object does not follow its allotted path but just goes straight from the start to the end point, it's almost certainly because you have not snapped the object to the line properly at one end or the other. Check the tween Properties and make sure that Snap is on, then repeat steps 8 and 9. It may help to zoom in closer so that you can locate the object more accurately.

5.4 Mask layers

Normal layers are transparent; mask layers are opaque – except for the 'hole' that you make in them. The hole can expand, contract or move over the surface, to reveal parts of the underlying images. It's a simple concept, and simple to put into practice.

The hole in the mask is produced by the stroke and fill of a shape – any shape. This can be resized or reshaped by the standard shape tweening routines, or it can be moved over the underlying image using motion tweens. (Though you cannot add a motion guide to a mask layer, so if you want complex motion, you will have to set up a series of straight line movements.) Once the mask shape has been created and animated – and not before – it is turned into a mask. The shape becomes transparent and the unused parts of the layer become opaque.

A static mask layer can have any number of separate holes, but if you want to animate the mask, there can only be a single masking object. However, this can be made up of several shapes, as long as they are all grouped into one object.

For the next exercise you need some kind of image on the stage to run the mask over. You could draw something, or import a picture from file. That's what I've done. Flash can handle all common image formats, and importing is simple.

To *import an image to make a background:*

1 Start a new document.

2 On the **File** menu, point to **Import** and select **Import to Stage...**

3 At the **Import** dialog box, locate the picture file.

4 Use **Free Transform** to adjust the image to fit the stage.

To *create an animated mask:*

1 Create a new layer.

2 For a shape-changing animation, draw a single filled shape where you want the initial hole to be. Completely cover the image if you want it all to be visible at the start.

   For a motion-based animation, draw the initial set of holes and group them into one object.

After creating the hole shape, the layer is turned into a mask.

In this simple mask, the hole shape expands to reveal the image.

3 Create keyframes for both layers, at a suitable place down the Timeline.

4 Transform or move the mask object to its end state, then set up shape or motion tweens, as appropriate.

5 Right-click on the mask layer and select **Mask** on the menu, to place a tick by it. The display should invert, with the mask object turning into a hole and the rest of the layer becoming the current background colour.

6 Play the animation to check the effects.

7 If you need to adjust the animation, either turn off the **Mask** setting, or unlock the layer.

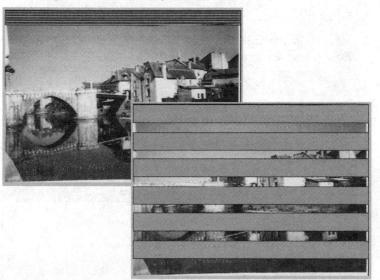

A multiple-hole mask, animated with motion tweens, but using the Free Transform tool to enlarge the mask object.

5.5 Timeline effects

The Timeline effects are a mixture of static display effects and animations. They are included in this chapter because they work through the layer system.

There are three sets of effects:

- **Assistants – Copy to Grid** and **Distributed Duplicate,** both of which produce multiple, *static,* images.

- **Effects – Blur, Expand** and **Explode** are animations; **Shadow** is a static effect. All are what you'd expect from the names.

- **Transform/Transition** are animations. With **Transform** you can move, rotate, transform and recolour an object, just as you can using the techniques covered in the last chapter, but with this it's all done in one operation. **Transition**s are ready-made fade and wipe effects.

The basic technique is the same for all effects.

1 Select the object to which the effect is to be applied.

2 Start from the **Insert** or right-click menu, point to **Timeline Effects** and select the one you want.

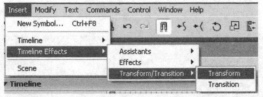

3 You will see a dialog box where the effect's options are set.

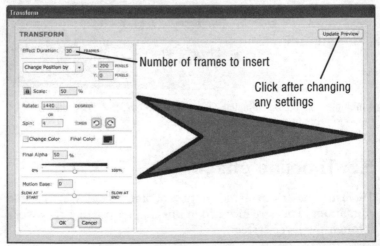

All the dialog boxes have the same basic layout.

4 After you have clicked **OK**, the effect will be applied. (It may take Flash a few seconds to work it out.) The object will be taken into a new layer (unless it was the only object in its layer), and the layer will be renamed to indicate the effect. If it is an animation, frames will be inserted into the timeline.

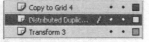

5 You can reopen the dialog box to edit the effect. Right-click on the object and select **Timeline Effects > Edit Effect** from the menu.

6 To remove the effect, right-click and select **Timeline Effects > Remove Effect**.

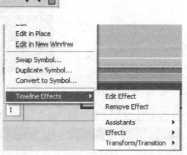

Visibility and the Alpha value

The Transform dialog box includes an Alpha setting that allows you to make object(s) more or less visible during the transformation. You could, for example, make something fade away as it got smaller, so that it appeared to disappear into the distance.

![Blur dialog box with Effect Duration: 24 frames, Resolution: 15, Scale: 0.5, Allow Horizontal Blur and Allow Vertical Blur checked, Direction of Movement arrows, and a preview pane]

Blur expands and fades an image. Experiment with the settings to see the kind of effects that can be produced.

COPY TO GRID

Grid Size:

ROWS: 4   COLUMNS: 8

Grid Spacing:

ROWS: 2   PIXELS   COLUMNS: 2   PIXELS

Update Preview

OK   Cancel

DISTRIBUTED DUPLICATE

Number of Copies: 7

Offset Distance: X: 40   PIXELS
                   Y: 20   PIXELS

Offset Rotation: 0   DEGREES

Offset Start Frame: 0   FRAMES

Exponential Scaling

🔒 Scale: 95   %

☑ Change Color   Final Color

Final Alpha   22   %

0% ———————○—————————— 100%

Update Preview

OK   Cancel

Copy to Grid (top) and **Distributed Duplicate** (bottom) are convenient ways to create multiple copies of objects. The result is in fact a single object. If you want to use the copies as separate images, the object can be broken up into its components using **Modify > Break Apart** (see below).

Stripping layers

If you feel that you need to do major editing on an animated layer – whether it is a mask or a plain moving object – it may be simpler to delete the layer and start again.

5.6 Distribute to layers

If you want to animate several objects, you can do it better if they are on separate layers – in fact, that may be the only way to get the movement that you want. However, if you have created your objects by breaking apart a compound object – like the multiples produced by **Copy to Grid**, or text objects (see the next chapter) – they will all be on the same layer. We could cut and paste them onto new layers, but there's a better way.

Distribute to layers will take a set of objects and place them each on their own new layer. They can then be treated just the same as any normal objects on normal layers. Try this.

1 Start a new document.

2 Create a shape – any shape, but not too plain or regular.

3 Use **Timeline Effects > Assistant > Copy to Grid** to produce a 2 × 2 grid of copies.

4 Right-click on the grid and select **Break Apart**.

5 The four objects should still be selected. If not, select them now. Right-click on the objects and select **Distribute to Layers**.

6 Select the first of the new layers. The object will be selected automatically. In the Properties panel, type values to move it to X = 10 and Y = 10 (this puts it in the top left corner).

7 Create a keyframe at about frame 30. Move the object across to the far right and create motion tweens in between.

8 Repeat steps 6 and 7 for the other three layers, but setting a different end point for each object.

9 Play the animation.

Exercises

1 Use a motion guide to animate an image along a curving path, in the middle ground between two layers. It could be a fish leaping out of the sea, a bird passing behind trees, or a car in an urban landscape.

2 Create a marble run animation, with at least three marbles. Use one layer for the track, and a separate layer for each marble (but sharing the same motion guide).

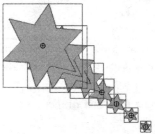

3 Use Distributed Duplicate to create 7 copies, reducing in size spread across the stage, of a shape. Distribute the copies to layers then animate them all so that they are stacked on top of each other in the final frame.

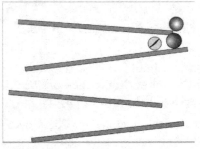

Summary

- A Flash movie can have any number of layers. The contents of each layer can be drawn and animated independently.

- Layers can be locked or hidden to prevent accidental damage.

- A motion guide layer can be linked to another layer to serve as a path along which an object is animated.

- A mask layer hides all or part of the layers beneath it. By animating the mask, different parts can be revealed.

- The Timeline effects are a set of ready-made static and animated effects that can be customized as required.

- The Distribute to Layers command will take a set of images from one layer and place each in its own layer.

05

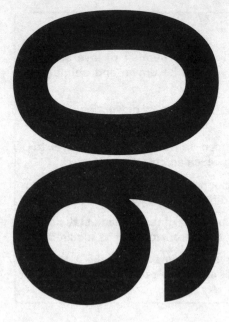

06

text

In this chapter you will learn:

- how to edit and format text
- about animating and transforming text blocks
- how to break apart text
- about using letters as shapes

6.1 Editing and formatting

You can work with text on stage in two ways: as text objects and character shapes. They are handled quite differently.

* A text object is a block of text which can be edited and formatted – and the formatting can be applied selectively inside the block. The block as a whole can be manipulated with the Free Transform tool, and can be animated in the same way as a grouped object.

* A text block can be broken apart into its characters, with each one becoming a shape, that can be manipulated in the same way as any drawn shape. Character shapes cannot be edited and formatted as text and cannot be changed back into a text block.

There are actually three types of text in Flash: Static, Dynamic and Input.

* *Static* is used purely for display and can only be changed during design time.

* *Dynamic* can be changed by ActionScript while a movie is running.

* *Input* can be changed by the user viewing a movie.

All three are edited and formatted in the same way, and we are only concerned with Static text at this point. We'll come back to Dynamic and Input text in Chapter 10.

To create and edit text:

1 Select the **Text** tool. The cursor will change to $^+$A.

2 Drag across where you want the text to go, starting from the top left corner. You will see a rectangle with a thin border, deep enough for one line of text in the current font size. There will be a flashing cursor on the left.

3 If you know how you want the text to appear, format it in the **Properties** panel. Formatting can also be done later.

4 Type your text. If you reach the right edge and keep typing, the rectangle will expand down another line.

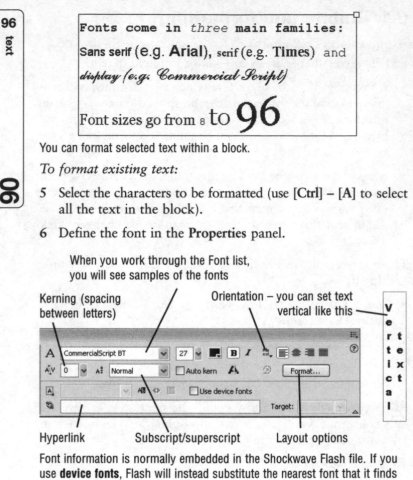

Fonts come in *three* **main families:**

Sans serif (e.g. **Arial**), serif (e.g. Times) and

display (e.g. Commercial Script)

Font sizes go from ₈ to **96**

You can format selected text within a block.

To format existing text:

5 Select the characters to be formatted (use **[Ctrl] – [A]** to select all the text in the block).

6 Define the font in the **Properties** panel.

When you work through the Font list,
you will see samples of the fonts

Kerning (spacing
between letters)

Orientation – you can set text
vertical like this

Vertical

Hyperlink   Subscript/superscript   Layout options

Font information is normally embedded in the Shockwave Flash file. If you use **device fonts**, Flash will instead substitute the nearest font that it finds when it is played on another computer. The SWF file will be smaller, but the quality of the display may not be as good.

Layout

The Format... button opens the Format Options dialog box where you can define the layout by setting the indent, margins and spacing between the lines.

Format Options

Indent:	0 px
Line spacing:	2 pt
Left margin:	0 px
Right margin:	0 px

OK

Cancel

Adjusting the text block

If you enlarge the font, the text box will increase in depth – not width – to accommodate it. You can make the box wider, and/or move it, using the text tool.

To change the width of a text block:

1   Select the Text tool, if it is not already selected, and click into the text block to select that.

2   Point to the box at the upper right corner. The cursor will become ↔. Drag in or out to change the width.

To move a text block:

3   Point to the left edge. The cursor will become ✛. Drag to move the block.

Move text block   Adjust width

In a distant galaxy far away among the
stars the forces of good are mustering for

6.2 Working with text objects

A text block can be selected with the Selection or Subselection tools, but once it is selected, all you can do is move it or delete it. You cannot resize or distort the block with these tools. However, the Free Transform tool works on text. A block can be rotated, skewed, resized in either or both dimensions.

Distortions

This opens up some possibilities for animating text. Try this.

1   Start a new document.

2   Select the Text tool and type a cheery greeting. Format it large and loud so that it almost fills the width of the stage.

3   Create a keyframe at frame 30 or thereabouts.

4 Go back to frame 1, and use the **Free Transform** tool to shrink the text box until it is barely visible.

5 Set up motion tweens in the **Properties** panel, turning on the **Rotate** option.

6 Play the movie. You should see your message spinning out towards you.

Typewriter effects

If you want to use motion or shape tweening on a text block, you cannot change its definition between the start and end frames – you cannot edit the text, or alter the formatting. If you wanted to make text appear gradually, you could start with it covered by a fill the same colour as the background, then either fade the fill away to 0% Alpha using a shape tween, or move the fill out of the way with a motion tween.

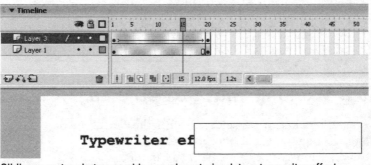

Sliding a rectangle to one side can almost simulate a typewriter effect.
(For best results, use an equal spaced font like Courier, and have the
same number of, or twice as many, frames as letters.)

If you want a proper typewriter effect – a hackneyed but still effective way to draw your audience's eyes to the text – you can do it, but not with Flash tweens. You have to create your own 'tweens'. It's a bit tedious, but sometimes you have to suffer for your art... Try it.

1 Start a new document.

2 Select the **Text** tool. Set the formatting, then type the first letter of your message.

▼ Timeline										

```
TYPEWRIT
```

3 Create a new keyframe at frame 2. Click back into the text block and type the next letter.

4 Repeat, creating keyframes for each additional letter.

5 Play the movie. If the characters are appearing too quickly, slow down the typing either by inserting frames between the keyframes, or by lowering the frame rate in the document's properties.

6.3 Breaking up

A text block can be broken into its individual characters. These are themselves text blocks and can be edited and formatted, if required. The point of breaking up a block is that it gives you far more flexibility for animating. Here's a little demonstration of some of the possibilities. It animates the word 'skiing' along a motion guide, with the letters moving independently. To keep the letters separate, we will put them in different layers – they will regroup automatically if you animate them on one layer. Substitute your own word and move it however you like. What is important is that you do things in the right order.

1 Type and format your word.

2 Use **Modify > Break Apart** to split it up into letters.

3 Select all the letters, right-click on them and select **Distribute to Layers**.

4 Drag to select frame 30 (or wherever) for all the letter layers and make it into a keyframe.

Drag the layers up to add them to the first guided layer

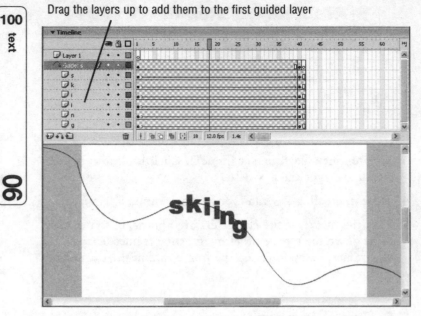

Letters are more flexible than solid blocks of text.

5 Right-click each layer in turn and select **Create Motion Tween**.

6 Add a motion guide to the first layer.

7 Go down through the other layers in turn. Select the layer
   and drag it up slightly so that the thick grey line overlaps the
   bottom of the layer above. The layer will be linked to the
   motion guide.

8 Draw the path on the motion guide layer.

9 Ensure that **Snap to Guides** is turned on.

10 Go to frame 1. Select the letters and drag them onto the start
   of the path. You may be able to do them all at once.

11 Go to the end keyframe and drag the letters into position.

12 Test the linkage by dragging the play handle. If the letters do
   not follow the path, go back to step **10** and make sure that
   they snap on at the start and end.

6.4 Characters as shapes

This takes breaking apart one stage further. If you break apart a single letter, it becomes a shape – or rather, the fill part of a shape. Why would you want to do this? Because you can do far more with a shape than you can with a text block. You can fill it with gradients or bitmaps; you can distort it by reworking its outline, adding new anchor points, corners and curves; you can draw on additional detail.

You cannot turn a shape back into a text block, so make sure that the formatting is right before you break the block apart.

Though the letter shapes do not have strokes around them, the fills do have invisible outlines and can be reshaped using anchor points, corners or curves.

A set of letter shapes selected with the Subselection tool to show the anchor points.

From character to cartoon – the shape is distorted, then given a radial gradient fill and some drawn detail.

You may find that these invisible outlines are not as easy to drag as strokes – it can be hard to tell when the Selection arrow is in the right place, especially on a dark fill. The Subselection tool can be easier to work with, and it is easier to activate the outlines by dragging a rectangle over the whole shape rather than trying to click on a point.

The last example for this chapter demonstrates the use of letter shapes, and gives further practice in the techniques covered in the last two chapters. This drops a word onto the stage, in a smooth sequence. You could make the shapes drop in random order, and perhaps bounce before settling into place. Play with the movements once you've got the basic animation working.

1 Start a new document.

2 Type and format your text.

3 Use **Modify > Break Apart** to split it up into letters, then keep the letters selected and break them apart again.

4 Select all the letter shapes, then right-click and select **Distribute to Layers**.

5 Repaint the shapes with a gradient fill and/or draw additional detail on them.

6 Select each shape individually and turn it into a group so that it can be animated with a motion tween.

7 Click on each layer in turn and check which shape is selected. It's simpler if the layer order matches the letter order. It may well be in reverse order, which is OK, but if any individual layers are out of order – and there's probably at least one – drag them into place. You may want to rename the layers, giving them their letter names – it helps.

8 Select the whole set and drag them off the top of the stage.

Drag the frames along the Timeline to stagger the action

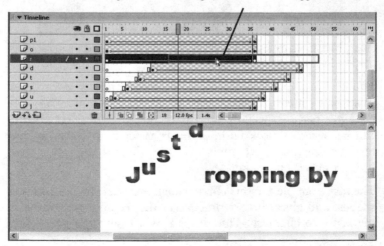

9 Decide how long it should take for each shape to drop into place and create a keyframe for *all* the letter layers at the appropriate frame. (I'm working on 3 seconds = frame 36.)

10 Right-click each layer in turn and select **Create Motion Tween**.

11 Go to the end frame and drag all the shapes into their final position. Check the animation with the play handle. They should all move down together. Let's add a ripple.

12 Select the second letter, so that its frames are highlighted. Drag the block of frames two or three frames to the right, so that its action starts and ends after the first layer.

13 Repeat for every layer in turn, moving each one a few more frames to the right.

14 Test it with the play handle. You should see a sequential drop, but also that the letters disappear after they've landed! The problem is that a layer is empty after the last keyframe. There is a simple solution. Select all the layers a couple of frames after the last existing keyframe, and create new keyframes there. The shapes will now be shown at their final positions.

If you have the time and the patience, you can produce high-impact text by animating letters separately.

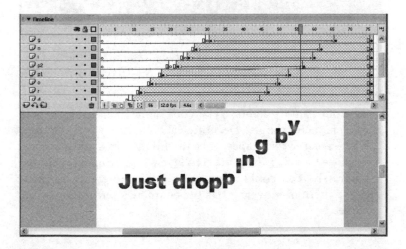

Exercises

1   Create a 'star wars' style movie intro, with text scrolling up and disappearing into the distance.

    Hint: The simplest way to do this is to make each line into a separate text object, on its own layer.

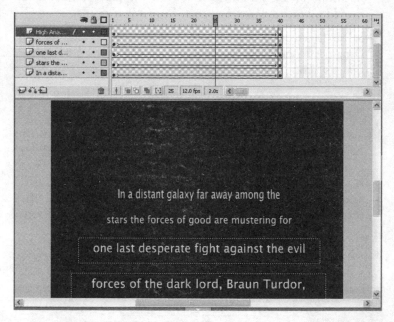

2   Bring four lines of text onto the stage – the title of the movie, or the welcome message to a web site – flying each one in from a different direction.

3   See your name in lights! Type your name then break it apart into character shapes. Decorate each character in a different way – recurve the shapes, vary the fill patterns, add dots and stripes – then distribute them to layers and bring on each one separately. You could use motion guides to create an intricate pattern of movement as the characters reform into your name.

Summary

- Text in Flash movies can be treated as text objects and character shapes.

- Text is typed into an outline rectangle. This can be resized and moved with the text cursor.

- Text can be formatted with the options in the Properties panel.

- A text block can be moved and transformed in the same way as a grouped object.

- A block of text can be split into characters with Modify > Break Apart. Using the command again will change the characters into shapes. These can be edited and distorted just like any other shape.

07 symbols and libraries

In this chapter you will learn:

- about symbols and instances
- how to create and animate graphic symbols
- about movie clips and how they can be nested
- about libraries

7.1 Symbols and instances

A symbol is a reusable element – static drawing or animation – stored away from the stage, in a library. A copy of a symbol, placed on the stage, is called an *instance*. Symbols are important for several reasons:

• **Efficient duplication** – if you wanted a bed of flowers, for example, you could draw one, convert it into a symbol then add as many instances as you needed to the movie. The main advantage of this, rather than simply copying the original drawing, is that Flash then only has to store one definition of the drawing, which helps keep the file size down.

• **Consistent copies** – all instances of a symbol are identical. An instance cannot be edited, though it can be stretched, skewed, rotated and otherwise transformed. A symbol can be edited, and any changes affect all existing instances of it.

• **Better animation** – symbols offer the simplest way to get movement within movement, e.g. turning wheels on a moving car, or flapping wings on a flying brick.

There are three types of symbols:

• A **movie clip** has its own multi-frame, multi-layer Timeline – in fact, you can do anything in a movie clip that you can do in a movie.

• A **graphic** can also be animated, though its Timeline is tied to the main Timeline.

• Buttons are interactive, and can respond to mouse movements and clicks. We will leave those until Chapter 9.

The Library panel

The symbols created in the movie are stored in its library, which is accessed through the Library panel. As well as each movie's own library, there are three libraries of ready-made symbols, such as buttons, that you can adapt and incorporate into your own movies.

• If the Library panel is not visible, open it now using **Library** on the **Window** menu.

7.2 Graphic symbols

Let's start exploring symbols by experimenting with some simple graphics. We'll convert a drawing to a symbol, place several instances of it on the stage, edit it, and duplicate it to create a new symbol.

1 Start a new document.

2 Draw a small object – anything you like, as long as it has at least one coloured fill. I used a matchstick man with a triangular torso.

3 Select the drawing, then right-click to get the context menu or open the **Modify** menu and select **Convert to Symbol...** (and note that [F8] is the keyboard shortcut).

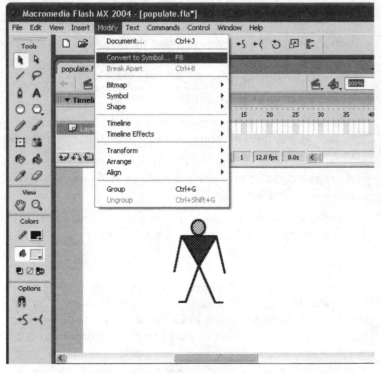

Starting to convert a drawing to a symbol.

4 The **Convert to Symbol** dialog box will open. Type in a suitable name, select **Graphic** as the **Behavior** (type) and click OK.

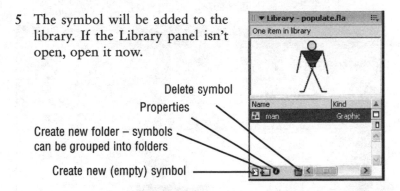

The Registration point is where the X,Y values are taken from, and may matter if you want to place instances at exact locations, or if instances will be created within ActionScript code. The point can be at the centre, corners or mid-sides – click on the little graphic to set the position.

5 The symbol will be added to the library. If the Library panel isn't open, open it now.

Delete symbol

Properties

Create new folder – symbols can be grouped into folders

Create new (empty) symbol

What you have on stage now is an instance of your new symbol. Notice that when it is selected, it has a thin blue outline. This is to remind you that, like groups (which have the same outline) symbols cannot be edited. Try to bend a line or drag a corner, and the whole thing will move. Try to add some extra detail, and the new drawing will fall through and land on the stage behind.

As with groups, symbols can be manipulated with the **Free Transform** tool and the **Transform** commands.

6 Click on the symbol in the Library panel and drag it onto the stage to create another instance. Transform it.

7 Create some more instances, transforming them in different ways and scattering them round the stage – leave a bit of space!

Editing symbols

Symbols can be edited, but not on the stage. You have to get them into their own editing window.

1 Double-click on *any* instance of the symbol, or right-click on one and select **Edit** to go into symbol editing mode.

2 The symbol name will appear in the bar above the Timeline, and the rest of the image will be partly faded out.

| Cut |
| Copy |
| Paste |
| Select All |
| Deselect All |
| ✔ Free Transform |
| Arrange ▶ |
| Break Apart |
| Distribute to Layers |
| Edit |
| Edit in Place |
| Edit in New Window |
| Swap Symbol... |
| Duplicate Symbol... |
| Convert to Symbol... |
| Timeline Effects ▶ |

The stage   The symbol

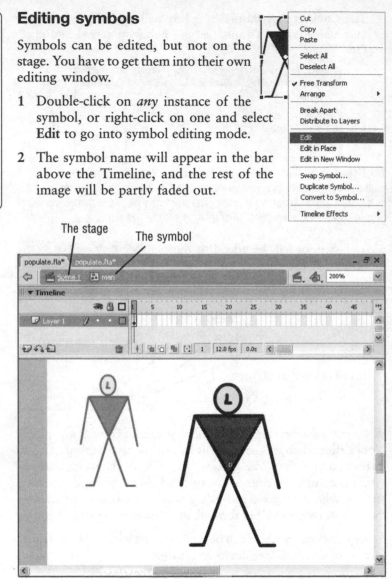

3 Change a fill colour on the symbol and watch what happens to the instances in the background.

4 Click on the <u>Scene 1</u> link above the Timeline, or use **Edit > Edit Document** to return to the main stage.

Duplicating symbols

The **Duplicate Symbol** command produces a new copy of the symbol – not an instance. Use it when a symbol will serve as a good starting point for another. If it's taken you half an hour to create a pink flower symbol, you could produce a yellow one in a matter of minutes starting from a duplicate.

To duplicate a symbol:

1 Right-click on an instance and select **Duplicate symbol...** or right-click on the symbol's name in the Library panel and select **Duplicate...**

2 At the **Duplicate Symbol** dialog box, type a name and click OK.

Duplicate Symbol	☒
Symbol name: woman|	OK
	Cancel

3 Right-click on the symbol in the Library panel and select **Edit**.

4 Edit the symbol as required.

5 Use your new symbol as normal.

How much time you save depends upon how long it would take to create the symbol from scratch

This looked better in colour!

Duplicate

There is a Duplicate command on the Edit menu. This is
different from Duplicate Symbol. It is basically a combined
Copy and Paste, and creates a copy of whatever is currently
selected, placing it near the original. It works on anything –
lines, shapes, drawings, instances, etc. And, if you use it on
a symbol in the Library, it will duplicate the symbol...

7.3 Animated graphics

An instance of a graphic symbol can be animated, just like any
other drawing. The symbol itself can also be animated, and if
you do that, every instance is also animated in the same way.

With a graphic, the animation runs in the normal Timeline –
movie clips are different as you will see shortly. What this means
in practice is this. If you animate the symbol over, say 10 frames,
you must extend your main Timeline over at least 10 frames to
see the movement. An example will make things clear.

Animating a symbol – I've redrawn my stick man instead of using tweens.

1 Take one of your symbols into symbol editing mode.

2 Animate your drawing. If yours is also a stick figure, you could animate it the old-fashioned way by redrawing the key frames. You can also use transformations to resize or rotate it. Note that if you want to use a motion tween to animate it, you must group the symbol now.

Symbols, groups and motion tweens

You do not have to turn a drawing into a group before you convert it to a symbol. However, if you want to animate the symbol with a motion tween, the object must be grouped – either before conversion, or before tweening the symbol.

---

3 How long is the animation? What's the last frame number?

4 Return to the Stage. You should see that nothing is happening. This is because you have not yet created time for the animation. Set up a keyframe at least as far down the Timeline as the last frame of the symbol.

5 Run through the movie with the play handle. You should see that all of the instances of the symbol are now animated.

7.4 Movie clips

The car drawing that you created in Chapter 3 can be the basis for this next demonstration. If you didn't make it or can't find it, take a few minutes to knock up a quick car image now. You only need one wheel, and here's why. We are going to convert the wheel into a movie clip and get it rotating, create a second instance of the same wheel, add them both to the car body and move the lot across the stage.

1 Open the car file, or create an equivalent one.

2 Take a wheel and modify it in some way so that it is no longer regular (if it is regular, you can't tell if it is rotating) – I've used an off-centre radial gradient fill. Group it.

3 Select the wheel, then use **Modify > Convert to Symbol**.

4 At the **Convert to Symbol** dialog box, type in a suitable name, select **Movie clip** as the type and click **OK**.

5 The clip will be added to the Library for that document. The wheel on the stage is an instance of your new symbol.

6 Double-click on the wheel, or select it and use **Edit > Edit Symbols** to go into symbol editing mode.

7 Place a keyframe at around frame 12, and create a motion tween between. Don't move the wheel – the only motion we want to create is rotation. In the **Properties** panel, set it to **Rotate** counter-clockwise, 1 time.

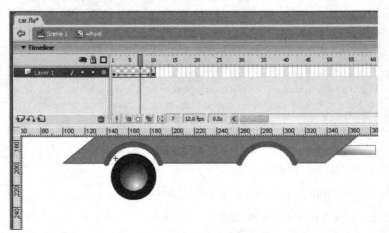

8 Use the play handle to check that the wheel does appear to rotate. If it doesn't, undo your way back to step 2.

9 Select <u>Scene 1</u> in the Title bar to return to the stage.

10 Add a second instance of the wheel at the back of the car on this layer.

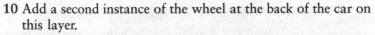

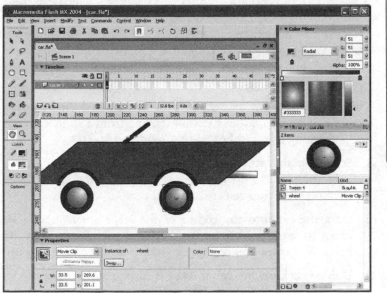

11 Select the whole car, body and wheels, and group it.

12 Move the car off the right of the stage.

13 Create a keyframe at frame 120 to give the car a few seconds to cross the stage. Drag the car across and off the left side.

14 Test the movie with the play handle and look carefully at the wheels. That's right, they don't turn! When you 'play' a movie this way, you only see the action in the current timeline. The wheels turn in their own timeline and that movement is only visible in the symbol editing screen and in the finished movie.

15 Use **Control > Test Movie** to see how it really looks.

16 The movement is slow and jerky. Running it across fewer frames will just make it fast and jerky. The solution is to increase the frame rate. Return to the stage and click on the background to display the document properties. Set the frame rate to 24 and test the movie again.

17 Save the movie – you'll need it for the next example.

Nested movie clips

A movie clip can contain another clip inside it – which can itself contain a movie clip, and so on ad infinitum. We can adapt the car movie to demonstrate this. We want the car to bounce up and down as it moves. We could use a motion guide to produce this effect, but it's simpler to create a clip of the car bouncing, though not travelling, then animate the clip across the stage.

This also demonstrates how to create an animated clip by copying a set of frames, rather than by starting from a static element and animating it in symbol editing mode.

1 Start from the last car movie. We need to remove the existing animation. Select all the frames from 2 to the end. Right-click on them and select **Remove Frames**.

2 Drag the car into the centre of the stage where it will be easier to work on. We need to separate the wheels from the body. We can no longer ungroup it, but we can edit the group.

3 Double-click on the car to take it into group editing mode. Remove the wheels with **Edit > Cut**, and return to the stage.

4 Insert a new layer and paste the wheels onto it.

5 Create new keyframes at about frame 5 and 10. The image in frame 10 should be the same as in frame 1, but lift the car body up in frame 5.

6 Create motion tweens on the body layer.

7 Highlight all the frames in both layers as a single block. Right-click on this and select **Copy Frames**. (Note that a standard **Edit > Copy** will not do the job here.)

8 Open the **Insert** menu and select **New Symbol...** Give it a suitable name – I called mine 'banger'.

9 An empty symbol will be created. You will be taken directly into symbol editing mode. Right-click on frame 1 and select **Paste Frames**. The three-layer set of frames will be copied into the symbol. Return to normal editing mode.

10 Leave that document open, but start a new one. Set the frame rate to 24 to give smoother animation.

An animation can be copied or cut from the Timeline to create a movie clip.

Insert > New Symbol creates an empty symbol. If you are not taken directly to symbol editing mode, select it in the Library and start to edit it from there. You can then paste in the copied frames.

11 The library and the bouncing car symbol will still be visible. Drag an instance onto the stage – or rather, just off its right edge. Use the **Free Transform** tool to make it a little smaller. We're going to set several cars running.

12 Set up a motion tween animation to take it across and off the other side in around 100 frames.

13 Add a new layer and drag another instance of the car onto that. Transform and animate as before. Add another layer or two of cars.

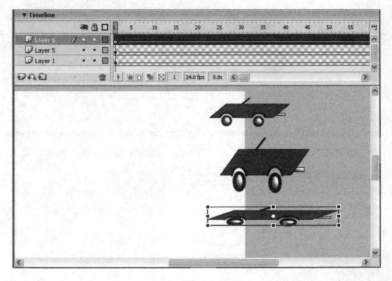

14 Test the movie. Are they all bouncing? Are the wheels all turning? (If they aren't you've done something wrong, or you are using **Control > Play** instead of **Control > Test Movie**.)

Using transformation to create different images is a bit of a cheat. We should really have produced different symbols for each car – and it wouldn't have been difficult. If you duplicate the existing car symbol, complete with its bouncing animation and rotating wheels, you are well on the way.

Note that to edit the drawing, you must first ungroup it – and if **Ungroup** doesn't do the job, **Break Apart** will. After redesigning the body in frame 1, you can copy it and paste that version in to replace the existing body in the later keyframes.

7.5 Common libraries

The symbols in the library of one document can be used in any other as long as the host document is open, and as any number of documents can be open at the same time, this means that you can copy symbols freely between your movies. But there is also another – and neater – way to share symbols, and that is to use the common libraries.

* Open the **Window** menu, point to **Other Panels**, then **Common Libraries** to open the submenu containing **Buttons**, **Classes** and **Learning Interactions**.

These are the libraries of ready-made symbols. We are not really ready to make use of any of these yet, but select **Buttons** just to see how Flash handles these libraries. It will open as a panel within the Library area, though its containing document is not opened in the main window.

Notice that the button symbols have been collected into folders. Double-click on a folder to open it. (Double-click again to close it.)

Editing common library symbols

When you use a symbol from a common library or from the library of another document, you cannot edit the original. You can edit a copy that you have dragged onto the stage, and that copy can then be duplicated within the document if you need more of the same. If you drag a new copy of the original onto the stage, you will get this warning.

- **Don't replace existing items** will apply your editing to the new instance.
- **Replace existing items** will create a new instance of the symbol and make the existing instances revert to the original.

Creating a common library

You can set up your own common libraries of symbols. A library is a normal Flash document – what makes it special is where it is stored. It must be placed in the libraries folder. And exactly where this is on your system will depend upon how you configured the installation. If you accepted the default settings you will find it down the path:

Program Files\Macromedia\Flash MX 2004\en\Configuration

To make a common library:

1 Open the file containing the symbols to be shared.

2 Use **File > Save As** to resave the document in the Libraries folder.

3 Check the **Window > Other Panels > Common Libraries** and you should see that it has been added.

To add symbols to the library from another document:

1 Open the common library as a document with the **File > Open** command.

2 Open the other document, and open its library.

3 Go to the common library and drag symbols from the other document's library onto the stage. They will be copied to the library and can be deleted from the stage.

Exercises

1 Create a movie clip of an insect or bird with wings that move – the creature itself should not move. Animate the clip along a motion guide to make it wind around on screen.

2 Build on the last movie to animate several identical creatures, plus some similar ones, made by editing duplicated symbols.

3 Create a common library to hold those of your movie clips and graphics which may be useful in other movies.

Summary

- A symbol is a reusable drawing or animation stored in a library.

- Graphic symbols can be edited, in the edit symbol mode. They can also be duplicated, and used as the basis for new symbols.

- If graphics symbols are animated, the action takes place in the main Timeline.

- Movie clips have their own Timeline, allowing you to create movement within movement. They can be nested to produce complex animations.

- There are three ready-made common libraries with symbols that may be useful in many types of applications. You can create your own common libraries.

08

graphics and multimedia

In this chapter you will learn:

- how to import graphics
- about graphic objects
- how to convert bitmap graphics to vector graphics
- about bitmap fills
- how to import and play videos and sound files

8.1 Importing graphics

Digital photographs and artwork produced in other applications can be imported into Flash movies. They can act as backgrounds; they can be animated – to some extent; and they can be used as fill patterns for shapes.

Flash can handle most common file formats, including the bitmap formats BMP, JPG and GIF, and the vector graphic formats WMF and EMF, amongst others. If you are simply using the file as a graphic object, i.e. not trying to change it in any way apart from resizing and other transformations, then it doesn't make any difference whether it is a bitmap or vector graphic. If you want to edit it, then the difference becomes important.

Graphic files can be imported directly onto the stage or into the library. Files imported to the stage are automatically added to the library, so the destination is not terribly important. As a rule:

- Import to the stage only if you want to use it there now.

- Import to the library if the graphic is only to be used as a fill pattern, or if you prefer to get all your materials together at the start of a job, rather than hunting for files mid-flow.

Note that a vector graphic imported to the stage comes in as a set of shapes. If it is imported first to the library, when it is copied to the stage, it comes in as a grouped object. A group is easier to handle, but a separated drawing is easier to edit.

Imported to the stage   Imported to the library and copied to the stage.

Dodgy imports

Flash can also, in theory, import EPS and PDF files, but note that EPS files can crash Flash. PDF files are broken down into their constituent parts – text blocks, line and graphics.

To import a graphic:

1 Start a new document.

2 Open the **File** menu, point to **Import** and select **Import to Stage...** or **Import to Library...**

3 At the **Import** dialog box, select the file(s) you want to import and click **Open**.

To import several files at once, hold down [Ctrl] while you click on them.

4 If you import to the stage, the file will open at its natural size.

♦ If you import it to the library, its name and kind will be listed.

Shrink ahead!

If you are producing Flash movies for web pages, file size is important, and graphics can add substantially to the size of a file. If you find that you have to shrink an imported graphic to use it in your movie, don't import it – yet. Work out what size you want it to be, then open the file in a graphics package and scale it down to fit and/or crop it to get it to the right size.

8.2 Graphic objects

Vector graphics, when imported through the library, and bitmap graphics, however they are imported, are treated as single objects and cannot be cropped or edited in any way – unless you break them down (see below). They can be selected, then moved or deleted, and they can be transformed with the ▣ tool and the other transform routines. What this means is that you can display them as static images, or animate them with movement, rotation, resizing or fading in or out using the Alpha settings.

Vector graphics behave themselves, and can be treated like any grouped object. Bitmaps are more awkward. If you try to set up an animation by defining the end keyframe and using the **Create Motion Tween** routine, the results are unpredictable – the tweens tend to get smaller, whether you want them to or not. The **Transform** dialog box gives more reliable results, and you can also use the Alpha effect, which works well with bitmaps. Try it.

1 Start a new document and import a bitmap onto the stage. Resize and position it as required.

2 Select the graphic and use **Insert > Timeline Effects > Transform/Transition > Transform** to open the **Transform** dialog box.

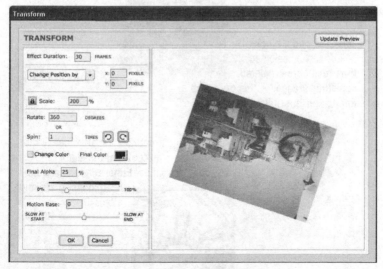

Click Update Preview to see the effect of the settings.

3 Set the graphic to fade to 25% Alpha after 30 frames or so. If you want to apply other transformations, define them now.

4 Play the movie to check the effect. If necessary, go back to the **Transform** dialog box to edit the effect.

8.3 Vector graphics

An imported vector graphic can be treated almost exactly the same as an image drawn in Flash. A graphic can be edited once it has been separated into its components (use **Modify > Break Apart**) though it will already be separated if it was imported directly onto the stage, as we noted earlier.

A couple of things to note:

• The images will probably be made up only of fills – no strokes – so use the Paint bucket to recolour. One of the side effects of this is that a continuous block of colour, however intricate it may be, is a single element and can be selected with one click. Compare this with strokes where a single click only selects as far as the next anchor point.

One click and a block of colour can be selected, then recoloured, deleted, copied or dragged – this opens up interesting possibilities

Clip art can sometimes separate neatly into the outlines – except that these are fills – and the coloured infills. Either of these can be used alone to striking effect

- When you break up an image and start to edit it, elements may disappear beneath other parts as Flash may not interpret the overlapping order properly.

8.4 Working with bitmap graphics

Bitmaps need work before you can do anything much with them – apart from using them as decorative pictures. Even putting a frame around a picture is not as straightforward as you might expect. (And if you want to do this, the trick is to use a shape with a Nil fill, and turn it into a group. You can then bring it to the front through the **Modify > Arrange** option.)

Trace Bitmap

The key to working with bitmaps lies in the Trace routine. This will convert the bitmap, where the colour of each pixel is individually recorded, into a vector image. It works by taking groups of pixels of similar colours and turning them into a fill. There are two variables there:

- 'groups of pixels' – how big is a group?
- 'similar colours' – how similar?

Obviously, the larger the group and the larger the range of colours counted as similar, the chunkier the image after conversion – and the smaller the resulting movie's file. Very high resolution, (i.e. 1 or 2) and sharp colour definition (less than 40 or so) is not a problem with small pictures as the impact on file size won't be that great. You *will* notice it with larger pictures. Flash will slow down significantly and may crash completely.

Explore the options, and see the effects for yourself.

1 Start a new document. Import a smallish bitmap to the library, and place at least three copies of it on the stage.

2 Select the first bitmap image.

3 Open the **Modify** menu, point to **Bitmap** and select **Trace**.

4 Enter the **Color threshold** and **Minimum area** values.

```
Trace Bitmap                              [X]
  Color threshold:  100              [    OK    ]
  Minimum area:     8      pixels    [  Cancel  ]
      Curve fit:    Normal      [v]
  Corner threshold: Normal      [v]
```

Use these options to
fine-tune the output

5 If you want to fine-tune the result, set the **Curve fit** and **Corner threshold** values – depending upon the nature of the image, these may have little effect.

The same bitmap at
50 threshold, 2 pixels...

...100 threshold, 4 pixels...

...200 threshold, 8 pixels

You have to decide on the best balance of resolution and file size. You may
also decide that sometimes a low-colour, low-res image works better.

6 Click **OK** and wait. High resolution, high definition conversion can take a few seconds.

7 Repeat for the other images, setting different threshold and area values.

Here's an idea that you might like to play with. After a bitmap has been traced, it becomes a vector graphic, with solid blocks of colour, and these can be selected and deleted. You could animate the disappearance of an image, block by block – or better still, reverse the animation and build up a picture by blocks of colour. Rolf Harris perfected this approach to painting!

Try it. You need a document with a suitable bitmap, traced fairly coarsely, say with a threshold of 100 and minimum area of 8.

1 Insert a set of keyframes, moving the complete image to the furthest frame.

Can you see what it is yet? Building a bitmap graphic.

2   Copy the graphic and paste it into the previous frame, then delete one or more blocks of colour.

3   Continue to copy, paste and delete as you work back to the start frame.

4   If there's still too much picture left when you get close to the start, insert more keyframes.

5   Test the movie and see what you think.

Note that this can produce huge files! It's probably not something that you would want to do on a web page.

8.5 Bitmap fills

Bitmap fills are ready to use with no special preparation – just import the picture to the library. Once it is there, it can be used as a fill – and it doesn't even need tracing beforehand. Initially, the image will be painted as rows of tiny thumbnails. Once it is on stage, the image can be enlarged, rotated or otherwise manipulated with the Fill Transform tool.

1   Start a new document.

2   Import two or three bitmaps to the library.

3   Select the **Oval** or **Rectangle** tool.

4   In the **Colour Mixer** panel, drop down the fill type list and select **Bitmap**. The colour palette will be replaced by a display of tiny thumbnails of the available bitmaps. Pick one.

5   Draw an oval (or any filled shape).

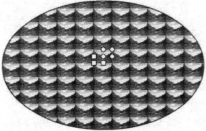

6 Select the ![icon] **Fill Transform** tool.

7 Click on any of the thumbnails in the fill.

♦ Drag the bottom left handle to enlarge the image in both directions.

♦ Drag the left or bottom handles to change the width or height only.

♦ Drag the top or the right handles to skew.

♦ Drag around the top right handle to rotate the image.

♦ Drag the centre handle to move the image within the shape.

If you create several shapes, all filled with the same bitmap, in one session, then the alterations you make to the fill in one shape will automatically be copied over into the rest of that set. If the bitmap is expanded so that it extends over several shapes, the fill in each will be that part of the image that is beneath.

Shapes created earlier with the same bitmap will not be affected, and later fills will all start from the standard thumbnail image.

You can copy a transformed fill from one shape to another. Select it with the ![icon] Eyedropper. The Paint bucket will be activated automatically – use it to refill other shapes as required.

Brushing with bitmaps

Whether you create the fill with a brush or a shape-drawing tool it looks the same and is handled in the same way. The only thing to watch out for – and after the first time you will be ready for it – is that the brush appears to paint with solid pale blue. This is replaced by the bitmap when you release the brush.

8.6 Video

A video file can be imported into a movie. Flash can handle all the standard formats, including QuickTime movies, Windows media .avi and .wmv files, digital video and MPEG movies.

Playback can be automatic, starting when the first frame of the video is reached, or it can be controlled by the user.

To import and play a video:

1   Go to the layer on which the video is to be placed and select the frame on which it is to start.

2   Open the **File** menu, point to **Import** and select **Import to Stage...** or **Import to Library...**

3   At the **Import** dialog box, change the **Files of type** to the video format, locate the file and click **Open**.

4   Work through the wizard, responding to the prompts to set how the video is to be imported – if in doubt, accept the defaults!

5   The video will be converted into a sequence of frames. If the existing Timeline is not long enough, you will be asked if you want to add more frames.

6   The video will play when its starting frame is reached.

♦   You can set up buttons to control videos – see page 144.

8.7 Sounds

Sound files can also be imported into a movie and played from their frames or controlled by buttons. The files can be in WAV, MP3 or AIFF formats.

To import and play a video:

1 Open the **File** menu, point to **Import** and select either **Import** option.

2 At the **Import** dialog box, change the **Files of type** to the sound format, locate the file and click **Open**. The file will be added to the Library and to the list of available sounds.

3 Create a new layer for the sound and select the frame on which it is to start. Press [**F6**] to make this a keyframe.

4 In the **Properties** area, drop down the **Sound** list and select the sound.

▼ Properties						
	Frame	Tween:	None ▼	Sound:	applause.wav ▼	
	<Frame Label>			Effect:	None	
					applause.wav	
					fanfare.wav	
Label type:	Name ▼			Sync:	Event ▼ Repeat ▼ 1	
					22 kHz Stereo 16 Bit 1.9 s 171.0 kB	

5 The sound will be visibly added to the layer, and will play when its starting frame is reached.

▼ Timeline										
	🎬 🔒 ☐	1	5	10	15	20	25	30	35	40
📕 Layer 2	/ • • ☐									
📂 Layer 1	• • ☐									
🗑 🎬 🗓	🟩	↓ 🖿 🖿 🖿 [·] 7 12.0 fps 0.5s ◄ ▮								

♦ You can set up buttons to play sounds – see the next chapter.

Exercises

1 Import a WMF file of a vehicle and break it apart. Delete the coloured areas to leave only the outline. Animate it by adapting the image and using shape tweening.

2 Import a small portrait photo or similar bitmap. Convert it to fairly coarse vector graphics and try to animate the features. How difficult is lip-synching?

3 Import a bitmap file into the library. Select the Rectangle
   too, set the bitmap as the fill, and draw a series of narrow
   rectangles the full depth of the stage. Use the Fill transform
   tool to enlarge the fill image until it fills the screen. By creating a sequence of keyfames, and moving the centre of the fill
   image in each frame, slowly scroll the image across. Does
   this have potential for an interesting background effect?

Summary

* Photos and artwork can be imported into Flash movies.

* All imported files are stored in the library.

* An imported graphic can be animated and transformed
  in the same way as a grouped object.

* An imported vector graphic can be broken apart into its
  constituent lines and shapes.

* The Trace Bitmap routine will convert a bitmap into a
  vector graphic.

* Bitmaps can be used as fills.

* You can import and play videos and sound files in Flash.

09 buttons and behaviors

In this chapter you will learn:

- about buttons in Flash movies
- how behaviors can be attached to buttons
- how to write simple ActionScript
- how to make buttons
- about hyperlinks
- how to control video playback

9.1 Buttons

Buttons are the third type of symbols in Flash. A button is an object which responds to a mouse click, and which can have different appearances for when it is at rest, selected or being clicked. You can make your own easily enough, but there are also some very stylish ready-made buttons in the library. Let's start with those.

Library buttons

To use a button from the library:

1 Open the **Window** menu, point to **Other Panels**, then **Common Libraries** and finally **Buttons**.

2 In the **Buttons** library panel, open the folders to see the buttons.

3 Click on a button name to view it in the preview pane.

4 Drag a button onto the stage to use it.

Behaviors

A behavior is a ready-written ActionScript routine. There are around 30 of them, covering the more common operations, such as playing movie clips or imported videos, or handling Web links.

The behaviors can be found in the **Behaviors** panel. Have a look through the sets to get an idea of what they can do.

We can use the behaviors to set up buttons to restart and end the movie clip.

Add behavior

Remove behavior

Selected button

To control a movie clip with button:

1   Select or create a button with a suitable icon or label to indicate **Rewind/Restart**.

2   If the **Behaviors** panel is not open, display it now with **Window > Development Panels > Behaviors**.

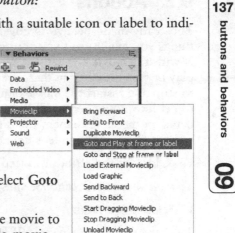

3   Click 🔩 the **Add Behavior** button, to drop down the list of options. Point to **Movieclip**, then select **Goto and Play at frame or label**.

4   At the dialog box, select the movie to play – **_root** for the whole movie – and the frame at which to start ('1').

Goto and Play at frame or label

Choose the movie clip that you want to begin playing:

this

🎬 _root
⊞ 🎬 (banger)
⊞ 🎬 car1
⊞ 🎬 car2

⦿ Relative   ○ Absolute

Enter the frame number or frame label at which the movie clip should start playing. To start from the beginning, type '1':

1|

OK   Cancel

5   Repeat the steps to set up a **Goto and Stop** button, stopping on the last frame of your movie.

•   A clip must have an instance name to be controlled in this way. If it hasn't been named in the Properties panel during the design stage, you can name it while adding the behavior.

•   Note that if you have movie clips within clips, you can stop an inner one while its containing clip continues to run.

9.2 Actions

The ready-made behaviors cover only a small fraction of the things you might want your buttons to do. An obvious example is with the movie clip set – you can go to a selected frame and play or stop the clip, but there are no options to allow the viewer to stop and restart the movie at any point. To do this, you have to get into ActionScript. We'll be looking at this in a little more detail in the next chapter, but single instruction scripts can be written very simply, so let's have a quick look at them now.

First, look at the script produced by adding a behavior.

To view a button's ActionScript:

1   Select the button.

2   Open the **Actions** panel. (If it is not visible, use **Window > Development Panels > Actions** to display it.)

3   The script will be displayed in the right-hand pane.

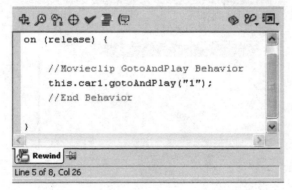

The grey lines starting '//... are comments. They don't do anything except help to explain the code. There are three lines of active code.

```
on (release) {
```

`release` is the event which will trigger the action. The { bracket at the end of the line marks the start of the code to be performed.

```
this.car1.gotoandPlay("1");
```

This identifies the movie to be played, and the frame at which to start.

this says that it is within the current document;

car1 is the name of the movie clip.

gotoandPlay is the action, and

("1") is the frame number.

The final line contains } the closing bracket.

You can soon learn the main keywords and how to use them, so that you can type your code from scratch, but you don't need to start from scratch. The keywords for the events and actions are stored in the Actions panel and can be simply selected and dropped into your code. Try it! Add **Play** and **Stop** buttons to your movie.

To add a simple script to a button:

1 Create or add a button with a suitable icon or label for **Play**.

2 Open the **Actions** panel.

3 In the code pane, type 'on ('

4 A list of possible events will appear. Select **release** and press **[Enter]**. The word will be added to the code.

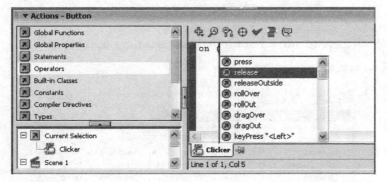

5 Complete the line by typing) a bracket to enclose release, and { an opening curly bracket.

6 In the **Actions** list to the left, double-click on **Global Functions** to open that set, then double-click the **Timeline Control** to open its set.

7 Select **play** and drag it into the code window. Notice that there are empty brackets after **play**(). These should be left

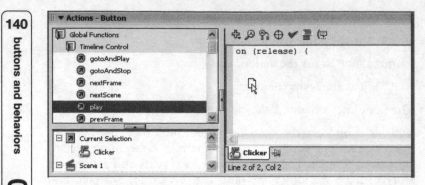

empty. Some action keywords must have parameters written into the brackets; others have no parameters. **play**() doesn't.

8 Add } a closing curly bracket on the line below.

```
on (release) {
    play();
}
```

```
Clicker
```

9 Repeat to add a button that contains the **stop**() action.

10 Test the movie.

Global Functions ▶	Timeline Control ▶	gotoAndPlay Esc+gp
Global Properties ▶	Browser/Network ▶	gotoAndStop Esc+gs
Statements ▶	Movie Clip Control ▶	nextFrame Esc+nf
Operators ▶	Printing Functions ▶	nextScene Esc+ns
Built-in Classes ▶	Miscellaneous Functions ▶	play Esc+pl
Constants ▶	Mathematical Functions ▶	prevFrame Esc+pf
Compiler Directives ▶	Conversion Functions ▶	prevScene Esc+ps
Types ▶		stop Esc+st
Deprecated ▶		stopAllSounds Esc+ss
Components ▶		

Actions can also be selected from the menu which drops down from the 🔧 Add Behavior button in the code window.

9.3 Making a button

If you don't like the buttons in the library, you can make your own. It doesn't have to be 'button-shaped', and it doesn't have to have a label or an icon – but these things help to alert your viewers that it is a button.

To make a button:

1 Create your basic button design – typically a filled shape with a label on top.

• If you are adding text to a button, it must be Static text – you cannot click on a Dynamic or Input text box, even when it is turned into a button.

2 Select the shape and its label, press [F8] or use **Modify > Convert to Symbol** and select **Button** as the **Behavior**.

3 If you want the appearance of the button to change as it is clicked, double-click on it to go into symbol editing mode. You will see that it has four frames: **Up**, **Over**, **Down** and **Hit** to match the four possible states.

    To redefine the appearance for any of these, select the frame, press [F6] and recolour or otherwise change the button.

4 The button can be used in exactly the same way as those from the library.

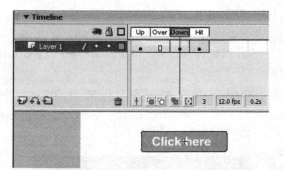

Simply changing the colour of the text is enough to indicate to your user that the button has been clicked.

9.4 Hyperlinks

In among the ready-made behaviors is one to add a hyperlink.
In HTML or in any Office document, you can create a link on
any piece of text. It's not quite that simple in Flash. If you want
to link on text, it must be a separate text block, and you must
convert it to a button or movie clip before you can add a link.

To add a hyperlink:

1 Create or select a suitable button or clip to hold the link.

2 Click 🔷 the **Add Behavior** button. Point to **Web**, and select
  Go to Web Page.

3 At the **Go to URL** dialog box, type in the address. (And just
  in case you want to link to Macromedia, the address will be
  already there for you.)

4 The **Open in** options define the page, or frame in which the
  new page will be displayed:

_self   the new page will replace the current page.

_parent   in a framed window, the link is in an inner frame,
         and the new page will be shown in the frame that
         encloses this.

_blank   opens a new window to display the new page.

_top   in a framed window, the new page will replace the
         entire framed display.

5 Click **OK** to close the dialog box.

6 Go online and test the movie.

9.5 Playing videos

There are behaviors to control embedded videos, i.e. those imported into the stage. There are five possible actions: Hide, Pause,
Play, Show and Stop, and they all do exactly what you might
expect.

To control an embedded video:

1 Import the video to the stage.

2 Create or select buttons to handle the controls you want to
implement.

3 Select the first button.

4 Click ⊞ the **Add Behavior** button. Point to **Embedded Video**,
and select the action.

5 At the dialog box, select the video
and click **OK**.

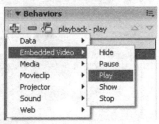

6 Repeat from step 3 for all the actions that you want to control from buttons.

7 Test the movie.

9.6 Sounds and buttons

You can add a sound to a button so that it is played when the button is clicked. In fact, you can add up to four different sounds to be played when the button goes up, down, or is rolled over or hit.

To add a sound to a button:

1 Import the sound to the library (see page 132).

2 Create or select a suitable button.

3 Double-click on the button to go into symbol editing mode.

4 Add a new layer to the button.

5 Select the frame at which you want the sound to play.

Sound layer

6 In the **Properties** panel, drop down the **Sound** list and select the sound to be added.

7 Check that the **Sync** option is set to **Event**.

8 Return to the main edit window and test the movie.

• The button can also have actions written into it, so that, for example, the sound plays when a movie clip is started.

Exercises

1 Take one of your existing movies with animation and add four buttons with behaviors or ActionScript code that will let the user start the movie from the beginning, stop it at the end, stop at the current frame and restart from that point.

2 Import a video and set up buttons to control its playback. Add sounds to the buttons, to be played when they are clicked.

3 Create a suitable button to carry a hyperlink. Duplicate and edit it to produce four more, similar, buttons. Add hyperlinks to them all to your favourite Flash sites.

Summary

- ◆ A button is an object which responds to a mouse click.

- ◆ There is a library of ready-made buttons.

- ◆ A behavior is a ready-written ActionScript routine.

- ◆ You can read and edit ActionScript in the Actions panel.

- ◆ You can write simple ActionScript code mainly by selecting from the lists of functions and methods.

- ◆ You can make your own buttons, with different appearances for different states.

- ◆ Hyperlinks can be attached to buttons.

- ◆ You can use buttons to control video playback.

- ◆ Sounds can be built into buttons so that they are played when the button is clicked or rolled over.

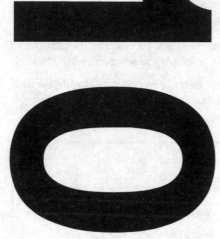

10 actionscript

In this chapter you will learn:

- about programming with ActionScript
- how to store data in variables and calculate with numbers
- about branches and loops to control the flow of the code
- about using components in ActionScript

10.1 Actions, events and frames

ActionScript is a large and complex programming language, and this chapter can only scratch at its surface – it needs a full book to be covered properly. Here we will explore a few key concepts and techniques so that you can add some interactivity to your movies. And if you find that you enjoy this side of Flash, then you might like to go on and really get to grips with ActionScript.

ActionScript is an event-driven, object-oriented language.

♦ 'Event driven' means that code runs in response to events, such as the user clicking the mouse or pressing a key, or the movie reaching a certain frame. The code is written in blocks, attached to frames, or to buttons or movies. For example, to make actions take place after the user clicks a button, you would write the code in a block that starts and ends like this:

```
on (release) {
    ...
}
```

The system will now watch out for the user clicking the button, and when the mouse is released, whatever actions are written between the { brackets } will be performed.

♦ An 'object' is a set of code which defines a structure, and contains 'methods' – routines that can control its interaction with the rest of the system. The structure may have a screen presence or may be an organised body of data that exists only in memory. You can define some aspects of the object – its properties – and you determine what happens within any method. The button is a good example. You define its appearance and the actions that take place when it is clicked. You do not have to tell Flash to create four frames for the button or how to pick up a click as it already knows these things.

If you have programmed in JavaScript, Java, Visual Basic or C++, you will notice features that are the same as, or similar to ones you have met before. You will also find some distinct differences, and these largely arise from the fact that ActionScript runs inside Flash movies, and that can have a major impact.

What went wrong?

When you run ActionScript, the system will check for errors and alert you to those that it finds – but it may not find all of them. If you have mis-spelled (or even used a capital letter instead of lower case – see later) the name of a method or variable, it may assume that you are referring to another one that it doesn't yet know about. Your code won't work and you won't know why. This is one of the little challenges of ActionScript programming.

10.2 Instances and properties

You may have noticed when working with movie clips, buttons and text objects that on the left of the Properties panel is a field marked *<Instance Name>*. We haven't bothered about this so far, but it is relevant in ActionScript. If you want to refer to an instance, it must have a name.

* To name an instance, select it on the stage, then type in a name to replace *<Instance Name>*.

Rules for names

Instance names may contain any combination of letters, digits and $. Spaces, punctuation and other symbols cannot be used. You can use upper or lower-case letters in a name, but mix them with care as ActionScript is case-sensitive. *myName*, *myname*, *MyName* and *MYNAME* are four different things. You may not use any of the words that have special meanings in ActionScript (to see a list of these, search the Help for 'reserved words').

Keeping names short and simple reduces typing errors, but the most important rule is that names must mean something to you!

Properties

You can use ActionScript to access and to change the properties of movie clips, buttons and text objects during runtime. The properties vary according to the type of object, but include:

_x   the position of the object's reference point in pixels from the right of the stage

_y   the position of the reference point in pixels from the top of the stage

text   the text in a text box

To refer to a property you must also identify its object, in the form instance.property, e.g.

```
UserName.text
```

This refers to the text property of a text box named UserName.

For this simple example you need an InputText box, with the instance name of 'Input', a DynamicText box called 'Output' and a Submit button. The stage should look something like this:

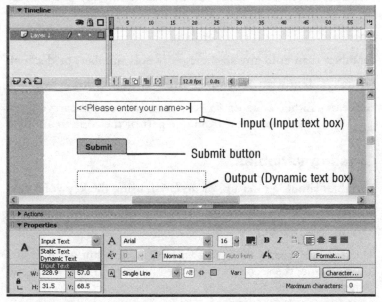

To set the type of text, drop down the list on the left of the Properties panel and select from there. The instance name field is immediately below this.

To add the code:

1 Select the **Submit** button.

2 Open the **Actions** panel, if necessary.

3 Click into the code window and enter the following code:

```
on (release) {
    Output.text = "Hello " + Input.text
}
```

4 Test the movie. Enter your name and click the button. What do you see?

10.3 Variables

Variables are named places in memory where you can store the data for use in programs. You can have as many variables as you need, and call them what you like – within the rules for names (see next page). The values can be changed at any point either by the code or by the user entering data.

There are three main types of data:

Number can hold any size integer (whole number) or decimal.

String Text written in quotes in the code or typed in by a user.

Boolean Either `true` or `false` – mainly used for carrying the results of a test from one part of the code to another.

Creating variables

Variables should be set up, or *declared*, using the keyword `var`.

```
var visitor:String
var max:Number = 500
```

The first line creates the String variable *visitor*, but without giving it a value; the second creates the Number variable *max*, and assigns 500 to it.

You can also set up a variable at any point in a script by simply assigning a value to it:

```
x = -99
message = "Thank you for calling"
```

These lines set up a variable called *x* with a value of –99, and one called *message* holding the string "Thank you for calling".

Variable names

The basic rules for variable names are the same as those for object names, though the convention is to use capitals only at the start of following words in a multi-word name.

```
ageLimit = 18
sex = "M"
var VATdue
```

Assigning values

To assign a value to a variable, use code of this pattern:

```
variable = value
```

The value can be:

* a literal – some text, or a number, or the words *true*, *false* (with Boolean variables);

* another variable;

* a calculation or other expression;

* a function or method that produces a value.

Scope of variables

A variable declared inside a function, only exists in that function. If you want to be able to read or change the value in a variable from different parts of the code, declare the variable at the top of the code in a frame.

10.4 Operators

In ActionScript there are seven arithmetic operators:

+	addition	–	subtraction
*	multiplication	/	division
%	modulus		
++	increment	--	decrement

The first four are used in the same way as in normal arithmetic.

% (modulus) gives you the remainder from integer division, e.g.

```
14 % 4 = 2
```

i.e. 14 divided by 4 produces 3, with a remainder of 2.

++ and -- increase or decrease the value of a variable by 1. e.g.

```
num++
```

This is quicker to type and has the same effect as:

```
num = num + 1
```

The operators can be used written before or after the variable name. If all you are doing is changing the value of that variable, it doesn't matter which form you use, but if you are using them in a loop and displaying or testing the value each time round, then when the value is changed may well matter. Watch out for this!

The values produced by arithmetic expressions can be used wherever you can use a variable or a literal value. You can write them on the screen, assign them to variables, or use them within other calculations.

Adding text

The + operator also works with text. For example:

```
username = "Jo" + " Bloggs"
```

username now holds "Jo Bloggs". (Notice the space before the second part of the name to keep them apart in the output string.)

This can be a problem. Inputs are through Text boxes and need to be converted to numbers, if that's how they are to be used.

Try this, you will need two Input text boxes, named *Num1* and *Num2*, one dynamic text box, named *Answer* and four buttons, labelled '+', '–', '*' and '/'. Write this code on each button – varying the operator in the last line to suit the button's label.

```
on (release) {
    var n1:Number = Num1.text
    var n2:Number = Num2.text
    Answer.text = n1 - n2
}
```

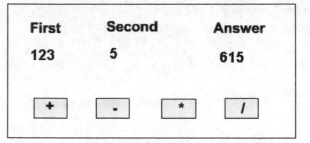

First	Second	Answer
123	5	615

```
+    -    *    /
```

A possible layout for the arithmetic testing movie.

Test the movie. Try with the values 4 and 2, and test the '+' button last. The results should be what you expect, except that '4' + '2' shouldn't make '42'. Flash seems to have forgotten that these were numbers. When this happens, the solution is to use the **Number()** function which converts the values to numbers.

```
Answer.text = Number(n1) + Number(n2)
```

Assignment operators

These combine an arithmetic operator with assignment (=), producing a shortcut for changing the value of a variable. Note that you can only use them where the same variable would appear on both sides. They look like this:

```
+=    -=    *=    /=    %=
```

and are used like this:

```
total += vat
num *= 2
```

These are the same as:

```
total = total + vat
num = num * 2
```

Operator precedence

Where there are several operators, the order in which they are performed is crucial. The standard rules of precedence apply. Multiplication and division are done first, then addition and subtraction. If part of the expression is enclosed in brackets, that part is evaluated before the rest, e.g.:

```
2 + 3 * 4 - (9 - 3) / 2
```

This first has its bracketed operation solved to give:

```
2 + 3 * 4 - 6 / 2
```

then its multiplication and division:

```
2 + 12 - 3
```

and finally the addition and subtraction to produce 11.

Pizza delivery! A worked example

1 Start a new document.

2 Set up the stage more or less as shown here.

The three text boxes below 'Number' must be Input text and named *LargeNumber*, *MediumNumber* and *SmallNumber*.

Below 'Cost' you need four Dynamic text boxes named *LargeCost*, *MediumCost*, *SmallCost* and *TotalCost*.

3 Write the following code on the 'Calculate' button:

```
on (release) {
    var lCost:Number = LargeNumber.text * 9.99
    var mCost:Number = MediumNumber.text * 6.99
    var sCost:Number = SmallNumber.text * 4.99
```

```
    total = lCost + mCost + sCost
    LargeCost.text = lCost
    MediumCost.text = mCost
    SmallCost.text = sCost
    TotalCost.text = total
  }
```

4 Test the movie. Does it work out costs properly? What happens if you type a word instead of a number? What happens if you remove the '0' and leave an Input box blank?

Pizza Delivery

Size	Number	Cost
Large 9.99	2	19.98
Medium 6.99	1	6.99
Small 4.99	0	0
Calculate	Total	26.97

Simple code cannot cope with the unexpected. It needs crash-proofing and error-checking, and there's no room to even start tackling those here.

10.5 Program flow

Program flow refers to the order in which instructions are carried out. In the examples so far, the code has run straight through a sequence, then stopped. There is a limit to what you can achieve like this – you need loops and branches in your code.

• **Loops** repeat a set of instructions a fixed number of times or until a condition is met.

• **Branches** take the flow off down different routes, depending upon the values held by variables.

Before you can do much with either loops or branches, you need to know how to test the values in variables. We'll get back to that in a moment.

Functions

A function is a self-contained block of code, identified by a name. It may carry out some kind of calculation and return a value, or it may simply perform a task. Functions are used to break a program down into manageable chunks – it's hard to read and debug a block of code larger than a page.

A function is *called* (activated) by giving its name in another line of code. After it has been executed, the program flow returns to the point in the code immediately after the call.

ActionScript has lots of ready-made functions, such as `play()`, which plays a movie, and `getProperty(object,property)` which finds the value of the specified object's property. (You can find them all, grouped by type, in the left-hand window of the Actions panel.)

You can define your own functions. At the simplest, a function is just a block of code with the header line like this:

```
function doTheJob() {
```

It must have the keyword `function`, the name and an empty pair of (curved brackets). The opening { curly bracket marks the start of your code, and there's a matching closing } curly bracket at the end.

You will see a function in use in an example code in section 10.7.

10.6 Comparison operators

These are used to compare the contents of variables with values or with the contents of other variables. There are six comparison operators:

```
==  equal to          !=  not equal to
<   less than         <=  less than or equal to
>   greater than      >=  greater than or equal to
```

Notice that the equality test uses a double equals sign '=='. The single sign '=' is used for assigning values.

Tests are enclosed in brackets, and typically look like this:

```
(x < 99)
(newNum != oldNum)
```

A test produces a Boolean value – *true* or *false*. Most of the time you do not need to worry about this – just use the test – but sometimes it is useful to store the result of the test in a variable, for reference later in the program, e.g.

```
var result:Boolean = (newNum > oldNum)
// store the test result
...
if (result == true)
// the same as using "if (newNum > oldNum)"
```

When testing to see if a Boolean value is true, you can miss out the '== true' part of the test, and it still works.

```
if (result)
```

is the same as

```
if (result == true)
```

Including '== true' can make the test a little more readable, but the shortform does make for neater expressions where you are testing several values at once – see below.

10.7 Branching with if

Branches make programs flexible, allowing them to vary their actions in response to incoming data. The simplest form of branch uses the if structure. This is the basic syntax:

```
if (test) {
    statement(s) if true
}
```

The *test* checks the value held by a variable. If the test proves true, the statement(s) are performed, otherwise they are ignored. For example:

```
if (balance < 0)
    Message.text = "You are overdrawn"
```

The warning is issued if the user has a balance below 0. Notice that as there was only one statement, brackets were not needed.

if must be in lower case. If or IF will result in error messages.

Comments in code

You can write comments into your code to explain how it works, both for the benefit of others and of yourself in a couple of months' time – it's surprising how quickly you can forget! Put a double slash // at the start of a line and Flash will mark it in grey and will not try to 'perform' it.

Calculating fees: a worked example

The following code calculates the annual membership fee for a club. Members are charged £50 for each sport that they wish to play; women get a £10 discount; members over 65 pay half rates. We can handle these conditions with four if statements:

if the member plays bowls, add £50 to the fee (initially £0)

if the member plays croquet, add £50 to the fee

if the member is female, take £10 off the total

if the member is over 65, halve the fee.

Before we can do those tests, we need some information. We will collect this in Input text boxes, then copy it into variables. The data entry screen should look something like this:

Crequeney Bowls and Croquet Club

Name:	<your name>
Age	<your age>
Bowls (Y/N)?	<Y/N>
Croquet (Y/N)?	<Y/N>
Sex (M/F)	<M/F>	Submit

Membership Fee

And the code for each condition will be like this:

```
var CroquetPlayer:String = Croquet.text
...
if (CroquetPlayer == "Y") {
   feeAmount += 50
}
```

The calculations are performed when the user clicks a Submit button, and we could write the code in its **on (release)** method. In fact, I've written the calculations into a function, and this is stored in frame 1. Why? Just to show how a function can be used and also that Actions can be written into frames.

Work through these steps:

1 Start a new document.

2 Set up a data entry screen, with Input text boxes named *Bowls*, *Croquet*, *Sex* and *Age* and a Dynamic text box named *Fee*.

3 Create a button and write this code into it. This calls the function *CalculateFee()*, which doesn't exist yet.

```
on (release) {
   CalculateFee()
}
```

4 Create a new layer in the Timeline, and select frame 1. This is where we will create the function – code written in frame 1 of any layer will be read as soon as the movie starts. Placing it in its own layer avoids it being affected by any changes you may make to the other objects in your movie.

5 Type in this code. Make sure that you spell all the names with the same Capitalisation. The // comments are there for your benefit – you do not have to type them in.

```
function CalculateFee() {
   // start with the fee at 0
   var feeAmount:Number = 0
   // copy values from text boxes
   var BowlsPlayer:String = Bowls.text
   var CroquetPlayer:String = Croquet.text
   var MF:String= Sex.text
   var AgeValue:Number = Age.text
```

```
// test values and adjust feeAmount
if (BowlsPlayer) == "Y") {
   feeAmount += 50
}
if (CroquetPlayer == "Y") {
   feeAmount += 50
}
if (MF == "F") {
   feeAmount -= 10
}
if (AgeValue > 65) {
   feeAmount /= 2
}
//copy feeAmount to display text box
Fee.text = feeAmount;
}
```

6 Test the movie. Try all the combinations, clicking **Submit** to work out the fee each time. Does it work?

```
Crequeney Bowls and Croquet Club

Name:              Ivan U. Mallet

Age                74

Bowls (Y/N)?       N

Croquet (Y/N)?     Y

Sex (M/F)          M          Submit

- - - - - - - - - - - - - - - - - - - - - - - -
Membership Fee     25
```

if ... else structure

This variation on the **if** structure uses the **else** keyword, which handles the actions to perform if the test does *not* prove true. The syntax is:

```
if (test) {
   statement(s) if true
}
else {
   statement(s) if false
}
```

For example:
```
if (total > 100)
   carriage = 2.00
else
   carriage = 5.00
```

The carriage charge is £2.00 if you spend over £100, otherwise it is £5.00. Notice again that the { curly brackets } are only actually necessary if there are two or more statements.

Let's see if … else in action. In this example, the user is given three chances to enter a password. If the correct password is given, the code takes the user to frame 3 of the movie, which is where it all happens, whatever it is. If the wrong password is entered, a counter is incremented, and if the user tries more than three times, the code goes to frame 2, where the movie stops.

For this example, you need a new document set up as follows:

• Frame 1 has an Input text box named *User* and one named *Password* – this should have its **Line Type** property set to **Password** (on the bottom left of the Properties panel) so that it displays only asterisks. You will also need a button with a suitable label and some appropriate prompt text.

- On frame 2, a keyframe, delete the text boxes and button and type the message 'Entry denied'.

- Frame 3, a keyframe, should just have the message 'Welcome'.

The code is spread over two frames and the button.

On frame 1, the code creates a variable to count the number of tries. The stop() function is there to prevent the movie playing frame 2 until it is told to.

```
var tries:Number = 0
stop()
```

Frame 2 is the end of the line for those who don't know the password. The only code here is:

```
stop()
```

The main code is on the button.

```
on (release) {
  if (tries < 3) {
    if (Password.text == "letmein") {
       gotoAndPlay(3);
    }
    // wrong password, try again
    else {
    tries ++
    }
  }
  // had 3 or more tries
  else {
    gotoAndStop(2);
  }
}
```

10.8 Loops

A for loop allows you to repeat a set of instructions for a controlled number of times. The basic shape of the loop is:

```
for (var = start_value; end_test; change) {
  statement(s);
}
```

When the program reaches this line for the first time, var is assigned its start_value. The statement(s) are executed, and the flow loops back to the for line. The value of var is then adjusted as specified by the change expression and the end_test is performed. This will normally compare var with a value, e.g. count < 100. If the end_test is not met, the statements are performed again, and the flow loops back until it is met.

The simplest type of for line has this shape:

```
for (n = 0; n <10; n++)
```

This sets up a loop that will repeat its statements a total of 10 times, as n is incremented through the values 0 to 9.

String methods

As well as demonstrating loops, this next example also shows the use of two String methods. The **String** class is a collection of methods and functions that can be applied to any String objects. The two that we are using here are charAt(n) which returns the character at position n (counting from 0); and length which gives the number of characters in the string.

This example checks that an e-mail address is valid – it's very crude, simply checking that the text contains an '@' sign. You could use the last example as the basis for it as it also needs at least three frames, with frame 2 carrying the stop() code and a suitable 'no entry' message.

On frame 1 you need an Input Text field named *email*, and a button. The code is written on the button.

```
on (release) {
   var address:String = email.text
   // the variable valid starts off as false
   var valid : Boolean = false
   // test the string one character at a time
   for (n = 0; n < address.length; n++) {
      // if '@' is found, the address is valid
      if (address.charAt(n) == "@" ) {
         valid = true
      }
   }
   // if (valid) is the same as if (valid == true)
```

```
        if (valid) {
            gotoAndPlay(3)
        } else {
            gotoAndStop(2)
        }
    }
```

Nested loops

Loops can be 'nested' inside one another, with the inner loop running its full course each time the program flow passes through the outer loop. It's a technique that you might use when working with a table of data or a two-dimensional display.

The next example displays a triangle of stars, produced by two for loops. The outer loop runs through the values 0 to 6. The second takes the value of the outer loop as its start value, so it runs 0 to 6 the first time, then 1 to 6, then 2 to 6, and so on.

```
for (var x = 0; x < 7; x++) {
    for (var y = x; y > 0; y--) {
```

The stars are created by duplicating a movie clip, named *star*. This is present in the movie, though off the stage. The crucial line is this:

```
star.duplicateMovieClip(newname,newdepth)
```

The duplicateMovieClip() method copies a clip, giving it the newname. The depth parameter sets its position in relation to other clips – you will remember that they can lie over or under each other, and that the position can be set with the options on the **Arrange** submenu. The method getNextHighestDepth() will give us the next available depth.

Here's the complete code. Write this into frame 1. Notice how the _x and _y values are calculated and set.

```
for (var x = 0; x < 7; x++) {
  for (var y = x; y > 0; y--) {
    var depth = star._parent.getNextHighestDepth()
    var newname = "star" + depth
```

```
        star.duplicateMovieClip(newname,depth)
        star._parent[newname]._x = x * 50 + 25
        star._parent[newname]._y = y * 50 + 25
    }
}
```

Test the movie. You should see something like this, though your stars may well be different.

How would you change the for loops to get the point at the top?

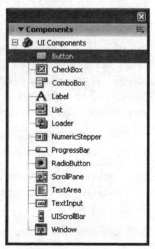

Loops in frames

If the code can be conveniently split over several frames, you can create looped action by sending the movie back to an earlier frame, and break out using a gotoAndPlay() to a frame beyond the end of the loop.

10.9 Components

If you are creating online forms or similar elements in a Flash application, you may find the Components useful. These include not only a button and a text input (which you can easily make yourself), but also a checkbox, radio button, scroll pane, combo box and other standard Windows elements (which you could only create with a good working knowledge of ActionScript). They offer a way to add extra functionality to your movies, without having to go quite so far into ActionScript.

To add a component to the stage:

1 Open the **Components** panel. If it is not visible, use **Window > Development Panels > Components** to display it.

2 Drag the component onto the stage.

3 Use the ⬚ **Free Transform** tool to adjust the size.

4 Give the component an instance name to identify it in ActionScript.

Parameters

Components are *compiled* movie clips, which means that they cannot be edited as can an ordinary clip, nor can you set their properties. They are customized and accessed instead through their parameters. These vary according to the component, but include things like *label* (the displayed text), *selected* (true or false), *enabled* and *visible*.

Parameters can be set through the **Component Inspector** or through the **Parameters** tab in the **Proper-ties** panel. They can also be read and set during a movie by Action-Script commands. The code has the same syntax as for the properties of ordinary clips and buttons. For example, TextInputs have the para-meter **text**, which is the text they contain. If you had one named *user*, you could copy its text into a vari-able with the expression:

▼ Component Inspector	
TextArea, <User>	

Parameters

Name	Value
editable	true
html	false
text	
wordWrap	true
maxChars	null
restrict	
enabled	true
password	false
visible	true
minHeight	0
minWidth	0

```
var UserName = user.text
```
To set component parameters:

1 Open the **Component Inspector** panel. If it is not visible, use **Window > Development Panels > Component Inspector** to display it.

2 Click into the **Value** field of the parameter you want to set.

3 If it is a true/false parameter, use the drop-down list to set it.

4 For others, type in the new value.

Components in ActionScript

Handling events with components is a little different from work-ing with ordinary clips and buttons. For example, you can pick up the click of a standard button with:

```
on (release) { …
```

This will not work with a component button. To capture a click on one of these you have to add an 'event listener' to the button, and write a click(evt) function into your code. It's a bit fiddly the first time that you do it, but after that, you just follow the same pattern whenever you want to pick up a click.

If you had a button named *OKbutton*, you would write this code into frame 1.

```
function click(evt){
    … // code to perform on click goes here
}
OKbutton.addEventListener("click", this);
```

If the button was named *submitBtn*, the code would be:

```
function click(evt){
    … // code to perform on click goes here
}
submitBtn.addEventListener("click", this);
```

The only thing that changes is the button's name, and – of course – the code that is to be performed when the button is clicked.

The next example is a reworking of the club membership calcu-lator. Comparing the two may help to show up some of the fea-tures of components.

Set up the stage as shown on the next page. Apart from the title, which is a Static textbox, all the elements are components. You need to name those indicated on the screenshot, as they are ref-erenced in the code. You should also give the same **groupName** to the two RadioButtons (for *Male* and *Female*) – this ensures that only one of them can be selected at a time.

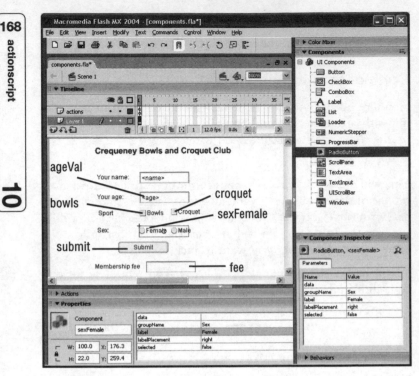

Create a new layer and type the following code into frame 1. (If you hate typing, you could cut and paste a lot of this from the earlier example – it is very similar.)

```
function click(evt){
    calculateFee()
}
Submit.addEventListener("click", this);
function calculateFee() {
    var feeAmount = 0
    // note use of selected parameter
    if (bowls.selected == true) {
        feeAmount += 50
    }
    if (croquet.selected == true) {
        feeAmount += 50
    }
    if (sexFemale.selected == true)
        feeAmount -= 10
```

```
        var ageVal:Number = Age.text
        if (ageVal > 65) {
            feeAmount = feeAmount/2
        }
            fee.text = feeAmount
    }
```

10.10 Drag and drop

One last example before we leave ActionScript. This demonstrates drag and drop, and also the use of random numbers. It is a jigsaw simulation. The pieces are scattered at the start of the movie, and the user can drag them into the right places.

1   Import a photo or other suitable image onto the stage. Use the Trace Bitmap routine to convert it into vector graphics.

2   It needs to be cut into pieces. Let's keep it simple and go for a 3 × 3 grid. Use the Selection tool to highlight the first piece, then convert it to a movie clip symbol. Name it *Bit1*.

3   Drag Bit1 out of the way and select the next piece. Convert this to a clip and name it *Bit2*. Continue to select and convert the remaining pieces.

4   Add this code to Bit1. When the clip is pressed, the drag starts; when released, it is dropped. Note the /slash before the name is essential here to identify the clip properly.

```
on (press) {
    startDrag("/Bit1");
}
// no name needed in the stopDrag() method
on (release) {
    stopDrag();
}
```

5   Copy and paste to add the code to all the other bits, changing the name in the startDrag() method each time.

We need to scatter the pieces at random at the start of the movie, and there's a handy random() function that we can use for this. It is one of several stored in the Math class, which is why its full name is Math.random(). It produces a random decimal value in the range of 0 to 1. This is not a very useful number, but if we multiply it by 550, the width of the stage, we will then have a random number between 0 and 550.

It will still be a decimal, but we can convert it to an integer value with the round() function. That brings us to this expression:

```
Math.round(Math.random()* 550)
```

which will be a whole number between 0 and 550, and that will give us the _x position for a piece.

6   Create a new layer and type the following code into frame 1. This will generate random values for the _x and _y positions and set the properties for Bit1.

```
var rndX:Number = Math.round(Math.random()* 550)
var rndY:Number = Math.round(Math.random()* 400)
Bit1._x = rndX
Bit1._y = rndY
```

7   Test the movie and check that Bit1 is placed at random. You are going to copy this code, so it had better be right. OK?

8   Copy and paste those four lines to produce random values for all your pieces. All you need to change is the Bit number.

9   Save your movie. There's hours of amusement for people here, trying to do the jigsaw!

I carved my picture into 20 pieces. As the code is largely produced by copy and paste, each extra piece isn't that much extra work.

Exercises

1   There is a set of Key buttons in the library. Add the Up, Down, Left and Right buttons to the stage. Draw an object – any image that would look good moving over the stage – convert it to a movie clip, and name it. Write code on key buttons to move the clip in four directions.

2   Adapt the last movie so that the object can be controlled from the keyboard. Use methods of the type:

```
on (keyPress "<Left>") …
```

to react to keypresses.

3   Design and create a sums-testing movie for children. It should display two random numbers and ask them to enter the sum – or the result of subtraction, multiplication or division. If the answer is correct, the movie should play an animation with accompanying sound. If it is wrong, then the correct answer should be shown. All the techniques you need for this have been covered in this book.

Summary

*   ActionScript is an event-driven, object-oriented programming language.

*   When using movie clips in ActionScript, they must be given instance names.

*   Variables are named places in memory where you can store the data.

*   The operators +, –, *, /, %, ++ and -- are used in arithmetic calculations.

*   The code can be made to branch in different directions, depending upon the results of tests.

*   A for loop will repeat a block of code for a given number of times.

*   Components can offer a simpler way to handle some types of actions. The values of components are held in parameters, rather than properties.

In this chapter you will learn:

- about configuring the Publish Settings
- how to publish a movie in a web page
- how to edit a web page to add your credits or other text

11.1 Publish Settings

The **Publish Settings** dialog box is used to specify the nature, format and other options of the output, and it should be checked before you publish.

* Open the dialog box with **File > Publish Settings...** There are three panels.

Format

Flash documents can be published in a number of formats, though the default setting is as a SWF (ShockWave Flash) movie embedded in a web page. When you run the Publish routine, files will be produced in all the selected formats.

The default names for all files are the same as the document name but with different extensions. They can be changed.

Click **Publish** at any time to produce the files, without closing the dialog box. You can then check the output and return here to adjust the settings.

Flash

These should normally be left at their defaults. If you select an earlier version of Flash Player or ActionScript, it will mean that your movie can be enjoyed by those who have not yet upgraded, but take care – some features of your movie may no longer work. Do check the output.

If there are images in the movie and file size is a problem, you can reduce the size by setting a lower JPEG quality.

HTML

These control how Flash sits within the web page. The key options are probably:

- If **Detect Flash Version** is on, anyone who doesn't have a suitable version of FlashPlayer will be offered the chance to download the newer software.

- The **Dimensions** can be set to match the movie, or be specified either in pixels or as a percentage of the browser window size – this is an option worth remembering.

- **Playback** is looped by default, but doesn't have to be.
- The **HTML alignment** sets the position of Flash within the page.

If you are adjusting the settings, you can publish from that dialog box. If you know that the settings are already as you want them, then you can publish directly using the File > Publish command.

11.2 Publishing to the web

First, let's see what you get when Flash publishes an HTML file.

Use **My Computer** or **Windows Explorer** to open the folder in which you stored the *.fla* file, and look for a file with the same name but an *.html* ending. Double-click on it to open the page in your browser.

You should see your movie – at the top left of the browser window with the default settings – and nothing else. The web page needs some editing.

If **Detect Flash Version** is on, there should be two other new *.html* files in that folder, one with *content* in the name and one with *alternate* in the name. If the file is called, *jets.fla* you should see *jets.swf*, *jets.html*, *jets-content.html* and *jets-alternate.html*. The main file is a check-and-redirect page, which loads the content page if the browser has a suitable FlashPlayer installed, and the alternate page if a new player is needed. If you want to add some text or other material around your movie, you need to edit the content page.

Editing the web page

The Flash-produced web page is a standard .html web page, and just to prove this we'll add some text – the 'credits' for the movie.

Instant HTML

Just in case you haven't used HTML before, here's all that you need to know to be able to edit the movie's web page.

An HTML document is a plain text file and can be edited in any word processor or text editor – use NotePad or WordPad. It contains instructions to the browser, telling it how to format text, and where to display pictures and other objects. It may also have links to other files and pages, and text to be displayed. The instructions are referred to as tags and are always written in <angle brackets>. Many tags work in pairs, with one at the start of the material to be formatted and the other at the end. These paired tags have the same keyword or letter code, but the closing tag starts with a slash, e.g. <h1> and </h1> tell the browser to format the enclosed text as a heading, style 1.

An HTML document has two parts: the <head> area contains information about the file, and is not displayed; the <body> area contains the material to be displayed and its formatting instructions.

If you need to know more, you might like to read my *Teach Yourself HTML*.

---

1 Open the document in WordPad, or whatever you use for editing web pages. There's some heavy-duty code here, which you should take care to leave well alone. Anything that you add must not intrude into any existing tag.

2 Add a title for your movie at the top, immediately after the `<body bgcolor="#ffffff">` tag. (Your `bgcolor` value may be different – it is the code for the background colour.) We'll format the title as a main heading, using the `<h1>` tags.

   `<h1>`*Your Movie Title Here*`</h1>`

3 Add your director's credits at the bottom, immediately before the `</BODY>` tag. We'll set a smaller heading format for this, with the `<h3>` tags.

   `<h3>`*Your Name Here*`</h3>`

4 Save the file and reopen it in your browser.

The movie web page after topping-and-tailing

```
<!DOCTYPE html PUBLIC "-//W3C//DTD XHTML 1.0
Transitional//EN"
"http://www.w3.org/TR/xhtml1/DTD/xhtml1-
transitional.dtd">
<html xmlns="http://www.w3.org/1999/xhtml"
xml:lang="en" lang="en">
<head>
<meta http-equiv="Content-Type" content="text/
html; charset=iso-8859-1" />
<title>jigsaw</title>
</head>
<body bgcolor="#ffffff">
<h1>Flash Drag'n'Drop Jigsaw</h1>
<!--url's used in the movie-->
<!--text used in the movie-->
<object classid="clsid:d27cdb6e-ae6d-11cf-96b8-
444553540000"
codebase="http://fpdownload.macromedia.com/pub/
shockwave/cabs/flash/
swflash.cab#version=7,0,0,0" width="550"
height="400" id="jigsaw" align="middle">
<param name="allowScriptAccess"
value="sameDomain" />
<param name="movie" value="jigsaw.swf" />
<param name="menu" value="false" />
<param name="quality" value="high" />
<param name="salign" value="rb" />
<param name="bgcolor" value="#ffffff" />
<embed src="jigsaw.swf" menu="false"
quality="high" salign="rb" bgcolor="#ffffff"
width="550" height="400" name="jigsaw"
align="middle" allowScriptAccess="sameDomain"
type="application/x-shockwave-flash"
pluginspage="http://www.macromedia.com/go/
getflashplayer" />
</object>
<h3>brought to you by Mac</h3>
</body>
</html>
```

The edited file should look like this – the new lines are picked out in italic.

Summary

* The Publish Settings dialog box is used to specify file formats and other output options.

* When Flash publishes to the web it produces a ShockWave Flash movie and a web page to contain it.

* The web page can be edited – though you must take care not to change any of the essential code.